THE
DOOR

Concepts create idols of God, of whom only wonder can tell us anything.

                        Attributed to Gregory of Nyssa

THE DOOR

FRAGMENTS OF
THE LOVE OF **GOD**

PAUL BAYES

DARTON · LONGMAN + TODD
INTELLIGENT ♦ INSPIRATIONAL ♦ INCLUSIVE
SPIRITUAL BOOKS

First published in 2025 by
Darton, Longman and Todd Ltd
Unit 1, The Exchange
6 Scarbrook Road
Croydon CR0 1UH
editorial@darton-longman-todd.co.uk

This product conforms to the requirements of the European Union's General Product Safety Regulations (GPSR).
EU Authorised Representative for GPSR:
Easy Access System Europe –
Mustamäe tee 50, 10621 Tallinn, Estonia
gpsr.requests@easproject.com

© 2025 Paul Bayes

The right of Paul Bayes to be identified as the Author of this work has been asserted in accordance with the Copyright, Designs and Patents Act 1988.

ISBN: 978-1-915412-26-3

No part of this book may be used or reproduced in any manner for the purpose of training artificial intelligence technologies or systems.

A catalogue record for this book is available from the British Library.

Printed and bound in India by Replika Press Pvt. Ltd.

For Katharine Bayes
(born 1956, married 1976, died 2024).
Memory eternal.

Forty-eight years of good weather,
Two old sticks leaning together.

Contents

Acknowledgements	9
Introduction	11
So there's this door	13
Picturing	19
Images and ideas and words	21
Doors and rooms and paths	29
All glorious within	38
The crowded threshold	47
Altitude	57
Thin air	59
All real living is meeting	70
In the valley	80
Speaking	87
Plain speech	89
The naughty step	99
On...	109
On love and anger	111
On being inclusive	116
On not being afraid	120
On Fr Bill	123
On finding a place to stand	126
On having sex on the brain	130

On conversion therapy	137
On being an ally	139
On ecumenism	144
Appendix	167
Notes	171

Acknowledgements

This book would not have been completed but for the support of my children, Honour, Sam and Philippa, and their families; of my publisher David Moloney and his team; and of a number of friends including Mal Rogers, Stephen Lyon, Jo Dolby, Mike Eastwood, John Inge and H-J Colston, David Walton, and Ken Howcroft. To them and to many others I am most grateful.

The lines in the dedication were written by my wife's mother, Liz Soley.

Unless otherwise noted, all passages of Scripture are from the New Revised Standard Version (Updated Edition), copyright © 2021 National Council of the Churches of Christ in the United States of America. Used by permission. All rights reserved worldwide.

Introduction

This book should have been in your hands at least two and a half years ago. My intention was to write it in the year after I retired from Liverpool as Bishop there. If I had done so, it would have been a very different book from the one you are holding now. I was aiming for a book written in the tranquillity which I believed retirement would give me. That was the plan.

But our retirement was not at all as we had planned or expected it to be. Shortly after we moved from Liverpool my wife Kate fell ill, and issues of life and death came closer and closer, profoundly impacting and shaking us, until only what was unshakable remained, and we could see even that only from time to time.

Kate's illness and her approaching death set us on a new journey, causing both of us to revisit and weigh a good deal of our inherited faith and its expression, and I found myself drinking from sources of Christian nourishment that I had not visited for a good while. You will read something of that here, if you have the patience to get that far.

Because of that journey, what you hold in your hands is very far from systematic. On the contrary it is a book of fragments. Many of the chapters can be read as reflections of a different world, more optimistic of the future, routinely seen in the harsher light of today's power-politics as utopian and woke and superseded. It may be so. But the ideas and values implicit in this book have nourished me, and I still hope for a world in which they may nourish others. So I offer the pieces here in the belief that they might reflect, in splintered fashion, aspects of the love of God.

And the direction of the book remains unchanged. It's built on the last sermon I preached as Bishop of Liverpool, just as my earlier book *The Table* was built on the first sermon I preached there.

Like much of the rest of the Church and the wider world, Liverpool Diocese has been through the fire since I left it. And in the present climate of the world, a book of fragments may be more use to you than any attempt at a coherent structure, since we're all having to build afresh in reliance on the grace of God, more like dry-stone wallers or the makers of mosaics than bricklayers or picture restorers. Perhaps, then, we need to find some fragments that fit our building or our picture, rather than reading about a well-proportioned picture or a building that someone else has thought up.

The door swings, and the journey continues, into rooms and on to paths. For me the journey within is to a small, unvarnished, empty room, with a presence intermittently felt, if always trusted. The road out is into anonymity, into the struggle for justice alongside human beings with no necessary Christian labels. The religious air I breathe has grown thin.

All this is new since I preached that final sermon, and yet perhaps it was prefigured there. If you read on, you can judge.

So there's this door

*A sermon preached at the farewell service
of the eighth Bishop of Liverpool.
Liverpool Cathedral, February 2022.*

So there's this door.
It's a simple door but it's well made, because it was made by a carpenter. The guy who made it is a poor man, but he's generous. He's given one to each of us, to open and close as we wish. He's given one to you.

It's a door made for people who come and go, who come in and go out, who come out and go in. Listen! The poor carpenter stands at the door and knocks. If you hear his voice and open the door, he will come in to you and eat with you, and you with him.

For Christians the Bible comes to us, and God's voice in the Bible. I didn't choose the readings today. They came to me. They are from those set by our lectionary for this evening.

In those readings, this comes to you.

In the Psalm it says: 'The King's daughter is all glorious within: her clothing is of wrought gold.'

And in second Chronicles, Solomon says, 'Give me now wisdom and knowledge to go out and come in before this people.'

And in John's Gospel the disciples say to Jesus, 'Now you are speaking plainly'.

For Christians the world comes to us, and God's love in the world, the world God so loved. We don't choose the world today. The things we face come to us. If you open the door you'll see them. Glory and love and joy. Poverty and pain and prejudice. Minorities pushed to the side. People frightened of difference. Exclusion and ignoring and hurt. Violence and damage and death.

And the Son of God sees it all. He sees us all, with our thin arms held out to the bare tree, wanting to live more abundantly. Let me go there, he says.

In this world the poor carpenter has given you a door, so that if you wish you can go in and come out before this people. Come in to the glorious presence of God who loves you. Go out to the disturbing presence of the world that God loves as well as you.

Open the door: come in. The Son of God has prepared a place for you, you are the King's child, all glorious within. Go out; speak plainly of Jesus and of justice. Go out and come in through the door, with the wisdom and knowledge God gives.

God has given you a door that closes, so you can go into your room and shut the door and pray to God who is in secret; and God who sees in secret will give the reward, God's real presence and God's blessing. It's a door for closing so that you may dwell within and know yourself to be all glorious, robed in wrought gold, clothed in bright raiment of needle-work, seeing yourself as God sees you.

But the Son of God goes out and comes in. And before He comes in, He knocks. And the door is not a door for closing when the poor carpenter knocks. Because it's only if you hear his voice and open the door, that he will come in to you and eat with you, and you with him.

And do you know what? He will not come in alone. He will bring his friends with him, they will all come crowding in, to the table that the poor carpenter made, the table which reaches into your own room, your own heart. And at that table you will sit with the ones who were shut out, and who are now included, as you have been included, all coming as they are, all robed in bright raiment of needle-work, all glorious together.

This line of scripture has lived within me for forty-two years: 'The King's daughter is all glorious within: her clothing is of wrought gold'. The first time I heard anyone preach it was in Sheffield in 1980, at the installation of David Lunn, Bishop Pete's predecessor as Bishop there, now three bishops ago. I have never forgotten it. Bishop David, whom I knew as a curate, used the text to lift the heart of his Diocese. He proclaimed to a poor Northern Diocese, to the Sheffield Diocese, that God saw them as precious – glorious and richly dressed, within.

And I proclaim that to you today, to this poor Northern Diocese, this Diocese which does not seek to be at the top of the Church but which has always sought to be at the front of God's mission.

As COVID continues to beset us, as the church is pushed to

the edge, as we work and pray and discern to find a way to be God's people in a new world, to make ourselves fit for the mission to which we are called, I remind you, you are all glorious within. God loves you. The King desires your beauty.

And I give you a charge today. I charge you to live in the security that comes from knowing that God loves you as you are, for your beauty. I charge you to remind one another that God sees you dressed in wrought gold, in bright raiment of needle-work.

That is the same God who stands at the door and knocks, and in the security God gives you, you need not be afraid. You can open the door to Christ and to Christ's friends, and welcome them all, and eat with them.

The poor carpenter will always bring his friends along. Among his friends will be those you would rather keep out. But the door was made by the poor carpenter, and it opens very wide, and it has a special threshold.

The world knows about thresholds. If you go on the Screwfix website it will tell you about the world's thresholds. It says, 'door thresholds are there to stop draughts and to protect against the elements such as rain and wet and cold weather from entering the indoor environment'. Screwfix thresholds are made to exclude elements.

But the poor carpenter's threshold is not there to exclude any element. It is there to help you welcome and bless. It is not a step. It is like the ground around the bare tree on the bare hill where the poor carpenter died. No one is special at that threshold, and no one is excluded. All you need do is hold out your thin arms.

In one of his books John Ryle, the first Bishop of Liverpool, pointed to St Augustine who said this: 'When Christ came forth from the Father, He so came into the world as never to leave the Father; and He so left the world and went unto the Father as never to leave the world.'

The gap between heaven and earth is healed in Jesus Christ. The threshold between heaven and earth is made smooth, and the door is opened. Heaven on earth in heaven, connected.

Jesus comes from the Father and brings the fulness of God with him; all of it. Jesus goes to the Father and he takes his friends with him; all of them, across the threshold and through the door, into glory.

Here's another charge, then, from your bishop. Stand at the door God made, the door you open as the carpenter knocks. Stand at the open door and speak for the excluded at the threshold. Stand there and welcome them in.

If you do that, if you stand there and welcome the excluded, you may be open to misunderstanding and to accusation and to struggle. But you need not be afraid. You are all glorious within; your raiment is of wrought gold and bright needle-work, rich and shining, because you are clothed by God. You're clothed by grace.

In today's reading Jesus says, I came and went. I came from the Father and have come into the world; again I am leaving the world and am going to the Father. And he says, I will tell you plainly of the Father.

That word, the word translated 'plainly', in the language of the Bible is *parrhesía*. His Holiness Pope Francis has commended this word. He has frequently said that only a church marked by *parrhesía*, by plain speech, by truthful speech, is a church worth having, and I agree with him. *Parrhesía* is the Bible's word, it's the Pope's word, it's the very word on which I spoke at our clergy retreat day last year, and it's the word that the lectionary has given me today.

It points to a way of speaking, and a way of being. You can see people who live that way. In the life of a man like Desmond Tutu, the greatest Anglican bishop of our times, you see one who lived that way.

In the spirit of this word and of those who live it, I invite you to walk this same way. Speak plainly. Fudge is sweet; but it's not a nourishing food. Don't just talk about God's love if God's love is not all you mean. Don't offer love unconditionally if later on there are conditions. Say what you think, and do what you say. Speak plainly and act plainly. May you be a people marked by truthful speech, even as truthful speech in this nation is respected less and less.

So there's this door and you stand near it, all glorious within. And you hear the carpenter, knocking on the door, and on the other side of the door you hear the murmur of his friends. Will you open the door, and face the draught and the rain so that he and the others may come in? I hope so. If it opens, open it.

In this Diocese of Liverpool we say, we're asking God for a bigger church to make a bigger difference, and we say, 'more people knowing Jesus, more justice in the world'. That's the swinging of the door, that's the breath of the Church.

As Solomon did, we ask for wisdom to come in and to go out. Wisdom for the inner journey and the outer journey. We close the door, we open the door; we breathe in Jesus, and breathe out justice.

'To make an option for the poor,' Gustavo Gutiérrez said, 'is to make an option for Jesus.' And that has been Liverpool's choice, and the choice of its bishops for half a century. Of Bishop David who wrote of the *Bias to the Poor*. Of Bishop James who wrote of *Justice for Christ's Sake*. In that tradition I have tried to stand. This going in and coming out. This breath of the Church.

As we breathe we adore our Lord. We say to our Lord and our God, all your garments are anointed with myrrh and aloes and cassia and you are anointed with gladness above your fellows. We say to our Lord and our God, it is your joy that is our strength. And God clothes us with wrought gold and with bright beauty of needle-work, with fragrance and joy, no matter what we wear on the outside.

Some of us wear bright beauty on the outside, as I did when I was clothed with gold and with raiment of needle-work when I entered this church all those years ago. I have worn this bright, beautiful raiment on behalf of all of you, as a sign that we are all glorious, as God loves and as God gives.

But wearing bright clothes, inhabiting a role, is something done for a season. It's a brief outward sign of a lasting inward grace. And the day has come when I must lay the bright clothes down, as the day will come when you must lay down what you in your turn have been given.

And when that day comes, when you are divested of your bright and beautiful raiment, and when it falls to you to go out in simple silence as you came in, I invite you again to hold fast to this truth, that you remain all glorious within. The love of God is what has made you beautiful and this love will never leave you, not in this age, not in the age to come.

And in the strength of that unfailing love I invite you again to open the door and to welcome your poor and lovely Lord, and all the unlovely poor ones he brings with him, to sit at the table with them, to listen to them, to make room for them, speaking plain words of thanks, and of truth, and of advocacy and of love to defend them and to bless them.

And I promise you that through them and with them and in them you will be blessing and worshipping our incarnate God, the poor carpenter, the one who enters your life through the door he made, the one who sits beside you at the table he made, the one you love, the one we love, the One who is love.

Jesus, may your name be first and last in all we say and do; and draw us to your Father in the power of the Spirit. Bring justice to victory. We ask this in your name, Jesus.

Picturing

Images and ideas and words

'And that is a vexation about the Gospels, you cannot be sure what was said, unless you are a fundamentalist and must believe every word, or have an infallible Church. Anglicans have less certainty but more scope, and can use their imaginations more.'
(Rose Macaulay, *The Towers of Trebizond*)

'People often suppose that imagination is Making Things Up. People who write even in a small way as I do know that there's an element of real discovery in the work of the imagination. You're generating new questions, new stimuli as you work.'
(Rowan Williams, in dialogue with Marilynne Robinson, *Christian Century*)

When my children heard that I was writing a book called *The Door* to follow *The Table* they rather cruelly wondered whether I was beginning the 'Domestic Furniture' series. 'What's next, Dad,' I was asked, '*The Hatstand*?' Well, no.

And yet for me, and for very many people, the royal road to understanding God and ourselves has always been through images. Images in scripture, Jesus' images of farms and homes and families, the images made by artists and craftspeople and writers though the centuries, and the images of my everyday life, even including domestic furniture. Tables, doors into rooms and on to paths, rooms deep in houses, paths through deep woods and into marketplaces. Images that can operate effortlessly on many levels. Images and what they evoke; emotion, and lives lived. Analogies, all of them; and if they work as images, then through them you catch glimpses of the mystery beyond all images.

Images matter, and yet in the end they do not matter. My working life was spent in a liturgical church, whose enacted images week by week fed me and those I tried to serve. But when (in my teens) I first began a spiritual searching, and now that I have stepped back from active ministry and re-ignited that searching, I connect more readily with the Church's underground stream – imageless prayer, manifest in so many traditions. I have been drawn once more to those whose worship is to sit in silence and to seek the Spirit of God in the silence. Indeed for the whole of my life this has been my native way of prayer, whether clothed in the language of contemplation, or in the repetition of the holy name of Jesus, or in the way taught by the Centering Prayer movement, or in the bare and gathered silence of the Quakers. Here, as Fr Lev Gillet says, is a way of praying that goes beyond the icon.[1]

Images and narratives on the one hand, stillness and silence on the other, have this in common; that they move beyond or without propositions. It is propositional language that leads to argument, to the contention for which 'poor little talkative Christianity' is infamous, or so it has seemed to me. We rarely fall out over parables or over silence. We fall out over doctrines and dogmas and definitions. I do not deny that these have their place, but it is not as significant a place as it has so often seemed, amplified as it is in the to-and-fro disputations of Christians.

After a lifetime of it I'm tired of contention, though I hope for strength still to engage in it for the sake of those on the edge of things. It is not least because of my weariness with contention that images and mystery and stillness are jointly at the heart, for me. And yet in my ministry, especially in my ministry as a serving bishop, I understood that words can't be dispensed with, nor contention either.

Archbishop Stephen Cottrell, whose ministry in the furnace of controversy I greatly respect, famously begins his sermons with an extended silence, drawing his listeners into a pool of stillness before he begins to speak. But begin to speak he does, as we all do; as Eliot says, 'I gotta use words when I talk to you'.[2] The use of words by the leaders of the church is necessary, even though it may be seen as a necessary evil. Certainly spoken and written propositions, essential though they may be, form the royal road to misunderstanding and argument.

My years as a bishop in Liverpool were for me the most crucial

of my ministerial life. In living them I felt a little closer to St Paul, who after listing the many serious physical hardships of his apostolic life, adds finally: 'besides other things, I am under daily pressure because of my anxiety for all the churches'.[3]

This is a season of trial for all the churches, one of many over two thousand years, and by no means the worst. These are more peaceable days than some in the history of the Christian people. All the same, in difficult times people find it easier to turn on one another, even to bite and devour one another, as scripture knows very well.[4] As a serving bishop with a clear view on some hot-potato issues, I was spared the physical beatings and shipwrecks and the other various dangers of Paul's account. But if you looked at the email inbox you'd find predictions of my personal, eternal shipwreck on the rocks of heresy, and every few days there would be an attempt to give me a verbal beating (usually beginning with a phrase like 'I'm curious...', moving on to 'as a bishop how can you possibly...?'). All this – what I said, and how it was heard, and the attempts of others to say more or to invite me to say less – all this swirling contention was the fruit of words, and usually of abstract ideas or laws, far indeed from images and from silence. Still, I had to use words when I spoke.

The churches are often in trouble, and the sort of 'what-a-joy' boosterism which denies that fact does not bless anyone in the long run. Nor frankly does the frequently-repeated trope that anxiety is, in and of itself, an ungodly temptation to be renounced by all true and trusting believers. It's true that Jesus took a nap in the storm – but it's also true that he cried out in agony from the cross. It's true that Philippians exhorts us: '... do not be anxious (in Greek, *merismate*) about anything, but in everything by prayer and supplication with thanksgiving let your requests be made known to God';[5] but it's also true that in 2 Corinthians, St Paul was under daily pressure because of his anxiety (in Greek, *merisma*) for all the churches. In short, life is complicated, and the Bible is not consistent. But you knew that. As John Macquarrie has written:

> ... people who think they have outgrown anxiety or that it is only a peripheral phenomenon may well be the immature people who have never been able to accept themselves and who comfort themselves with the illusion that is all is in order ... The fact that anxiety can sometimes reach an extreme pitch

where it becomes a pathological and disturbing factor should not disguise from us that there is a healthy anxiety or lead us to the opposite extreme of trying to suppress all anxiety or sweep it under the carpet. Anxiety belongs essentially to our being and discloses us in the very centre of that being as thrown possibility.'[6]

Anyway, my own anxiety for the churches was real enough. In Liverpool, which of all the Dioceses of England has the least inherited resources and is one of the closest to the financial cliff's edge, the wherewithal to support and resource the people of God and their ministers was lacking, and in a fractious church the readiness of some of the more comfortable to help the weak was not always as strong as the Bible suggests it should be.[7]

Spiritually, it's true, I was less anxious, given the faithfulness of God and the extraordinary faith and faithfulness of the people of the churches. This was true especially in areas of deprivation and difficulty, both in the city and in the towns and villages which make up the Diocese. They gave me heart. But I felt the pressure of anxiety, nonetheless. Seeking to care for the churches is a worry.

What can a bishop do, faced with these difficulties of sustainability and viability, and with the enormous diversity of the churches – a diversity often overlapping with their unwillingness to work with one another on grounds of theological, or geographical, or indeed personal preference?

One way forward is to reduce the Diocese so that it becomes as occasional a presence as possible. You can try to be an encourager with a pastoral eye on the leaders if they are prepared to receive it, and you can watch passively as each parish develops its own styles and purposes, helped by whatever networks it chooses to join. Many people urge this way of working on those with regional responsibility in the churches, and in the light of various scandals and cultural slumps these voices grow louder.

Such a hands-off approach can work very well. In Ezekiel's prophecy, inadequate human shepherds are sharply criticised, and by contrast the Lord says (in the REB translation), 'I shall search for the lost, recover the straggler, bandage the injured, strengthen the sick, leave the healthy and strong to play, and give my flock their proper food.'[8] This is a positive vision indeed. And any local church can be healthy and strong, provided that it has its own clarity of purpose, compellingly and persuasively expressed, and provided that it is well resourced.[9] In the absence of one or both of these provisions, churches will not and do not flourish, and at that point as a bishop you need to see whether anything you might do will help.

What more, then, can be done? Well, a magic money tree would be useful, or queueing at the door of the Church Commissioners. But in the absence of such a thing, or even alongside it, you gotta use words. The available resource is language, speaking or writing. The American journalist Ed Murrow said of Churchill in the Second World War, 'Now the hour had come for him to mobilize the English language, and send it into battle, a spearhead of hope for Britain and the world.'[10] To apply these words to the everyday work of a priest or a bishop may be to aim a little high for the course, and yet much of the presbyteral/episcopal task is the mobilising of words and images in the service of Christ. Not that one's attempts to do so are always warmly received.

In my time as a serving bishop, and it seems still more since I retired, a good deal of casual contempt has been lavished in the Church on the attempts of various Dioceses to sum up their purpose in a few words. For those who find this approach uncongenial, the boo-word 'managerial' is often used, a knock-down concept invoked to expose the foolishness of any such attempt. I have never been persuaded by these dismissive pronouncements, not least because of the comfort of the armchair from which they are so often spoken.

At any rate, in Liverpool we worked hard to sum up our purpose in a few words, developing it corporately and doing our best to secure ownership for it. We came to land on the phrase 'Asking God for a bigger church to make a bigger difference', with its subtitle 'More people knowing Jesus, more justice in the world'. I hoped that this phrase was congruent with the purposes of Scripture, as well as capturing the recent history of the Diocese under my immediate predecessors James Jones and David Sheppard.

I made the repetition of this phrase a key part of my own interactions with the churches, because it seemed to me to be a phrase which might align the different traditions and intentions of the churches in a way which set a good direction without being prescriptive. Later in my time in Liverpool I would try to emphasise the first two words of this statement: asking God. Asking God, so as to recall us to the divine initiative in all that we do. In the words of Martin Buber, words which I repeat in my personal prayers every day, 'The world and all of us who are in it exist by grace'.[11]

Along with this statement we tried to catch the human response to the gracious gift of the Lord in six words which comprised our Rule of Life. This too was a corporate process; the Rule of Life was re-iterated and improved multiple times in the Diocesan Synod to establish this agreement as widely as our structures permitted. So together we affirmed that as Christian disciples we were called by God and sent by God. Called by God to an inward journey, sent by God into the world. Called to pray, read and learn; sent to tell, serve and give.

This simple Rule, shaped in Synod and road-tested in our primary and secondary schools as well as in adult study groups and clergy Chapters, was offered in order to align people around the foundational practices of the church, while leaving each local community free to shape those practices in ways that made sense to them. Parishes, schools, chaplaincies and fresh expressions of the church were invited to take strength from these ideas and the resources that followed them if that was needed, and to make their own way with home-grown purposes and plans that nonetheless fell under these guidelines, if they had the strength. We trusted, then, that God will 'search for the lost, recover the straggler, bandage the injured, strengthen the sick, leave the healthy and strong to play, and give my flock their proper food'. I hoped that this pattern might be seen in Liverpool too; that the disparate talents, riches and prayers of several thousand Christians in a hundred parishes might be lightly but clearly aligned as part of one family, one Diocese.

Of course, the effect and influence of a bishop and of a Diocese is relatively weak. Compared with the day-by-day praying and yearning of local groups of believers, a Diocesan purpose is a fragile, often an imperceptible thing. In Liverpool I would liken it to the force of gravity, which is so weak that a child can lift an apple against the gravitational pull of the whole earth. Still, the attractional force of gravity can make a bigger difference than you might think. 'One can't help but think of a remark of [Nobel Prize-winning physicist Richard] Feynman's. He was giving a talk at a crowded conference, trying to emphasize the enormous (almost unimaginable) difference in strength between the gravitational and electromagnetic forces.

'Gravity is weak,' he said. 'In fact, it's damned weak.' (At that moment, somewhere in the back, a loudspeaker fell from the ceiling, crashing loudly to the floor.) 'Weak,' said Feynman — 'but not negligible.'[12]

Despite our best efforts, all this refining of purposes and statements may indeed have fallen under the cloud of a Godless managerialism, but we hoped not. Unlike the work of most management gurus our purpose began in dependence on God ('We're asking God for …'), without whose grace the bigger church and the bigger difference would either be quite unattainable, leaving us depressed, or would be exhaustingly brittle, leaving us full of an unholy self-congratulation.

Words can help, then; to my own mind at least, aligning statements are helpful in the life of the church. But compared to the power of image and story, statements are weak; in fact they're damned weak. Because abstractions will not motivate peoples' hearts. I write this in the middle of a General Election in the UK; the yawning gulf between the ability of politicians to make high policy statements and their simple ability to make human connections is more sharply defined in the news every day.

Not graphs and straplines, but people and images, and stories about people and images, are what connect. The pity is that populists and authoritarians understand this better than careful and able people, in politics as elsewhere.

In the Bible we see how clearly Jesus understood the 'stickiness'[13] of working through story and image, the simple fact that these things stick in the mind where abstraction slips away like water through your fingers. Images and narratives were Jesus' craft – everyday images and engaging, human narratives.

In my own orders-of-magnitude smallness I found this to be true in my own ministry. In my years in Liverpool I came across lots of people who remembered our Diocesan purpose, and a few who remembered the six aspects of our Rule of Life – but I found a good many more people who remembered the image of the table with which I began my ministry there.[14] And many of those who remembered the table also linked it to the statement, which was not my own but which I was glad and proud to borrow and use, that if you have more resources you should build a bigger table, not a higher fence.

It was with this scriptural way of engaging and this proven

modelling in mind that I made it my priority to share images and narratives with the Liverpool communities I visited. And at the end of that season, as my parting gift, I shared with the Diocese the image of the door that opens into rooms and on to paths. The fragments in this book spark away from that point.

In short, images and narratives speak to the depths of us, and subvert the contending mind. In my experience the controversies and disputes between Christians increase in proportion to the abstraction of the doctrines, dogmas, opinions which are nominally the grounds of conflict. I've yet to hear of parties and factions and schisms in the churches between those who see Jesus as the gate to the sheepfold, and those who see Jesus as the true vine; or between Prodigal Son Christians and Good Samaritan Christians. The mind has room for images and narratives which refract differently and which emphasise differently. It seems to me then that images and narratives largely bypass the besetting and unscratchable itch to be asserting, and for that reason if no other they should be valued as central to the discourse of faith.

Images, then. A door, then.

Doors and rooms and paths

What is the knocking?
What is the knocking at the door in the night?
It is somebody wants to do us harm.

No, no, it is the three strange angels.
Admit them, admit them.
(D. H. Lawrence)

Everything begins in mysticism and ends in politics.
(Charles Péguy)

The Bible is not a puzzle book, to be squeezed into pellets of doctrine by clever people, usually men, and force-fed to the rest of us. It's a picture book, containing letters and poems and histories and images and stories and all things necessary for salvation through faith in Jesus Christ. Most of all it points to the word of God, the One the Bible exalts, the human and divine Word, the sharer of images and the teller of stories, Jesus Christ.

So if you're called to preach the Word, that is to preach Jesus, it helps to open the book that points to Him. That's what I have always tried to do when preparing sermons, including the sermon which sets the frame for this book, the last sermon I preached in my stipended ministry. I took the readings that were given to me in the lectionary for that evening,[15] and I asked the question, What will these words provoke in my imagination, so that I can use my own words to point to Jesus, as these words do? And an image came to mind.

The image of a door stood for a very specific thing. I was trying to picture the place in each human being where the inner and outer life find their border. I saw that place as a door and a doorway, because it echoed for me John's image in Revelation, of the Lord

Jesus standing at the door and knocking.[16] That door. And in my imagination I examined and expanded that image to explore what it would mean to enter within, and what it would mean to venture forth. So the opened door presented me with a threshold and with many choices – to different rooms within, to different paths outside.

It was after I thought of this picture that I remembered the words of Charles Péguy: 'Everything begins in mysticism and ends in politics', words which have meant a lot for me for many years. So I laid this insight over the image, and saw the rooms within as the mystical space, and the paths outside as the political space. Riffing on that image and that idea, the sermon crystallised and grew. Preachers reading these words may find louder or more distant echoes in their own use of scripture and their own methods of production.

I agree with Péguy that everything worthwhile holds the dimensions of what he called mystique and politique. But I'm not so sure about his thought that the inner journey marks the beginning, and the outer road marks the end of a journey, or a project, or a life. Frequently for me decisions and choices in the political, interpersonal world have shaped my prayer and my awareness of God within.

The door is the place between the inner and outer choices, the place where as C. S. Lewis said:

> ... every time you make a choice you are turning the central part of you, the part of you that chooses, into something a little different from what it was before. And taking your life as a whole, with all your innumerable choices, all your life long you are slowly turning this central thing either into a heavenly creature or into a hellish creature ... Each of us at each moment is progressing to the one state or the other.[17]

An important place, then, and yet often a commonplace one. The door itself becomes familiar as you use it, coming in and going out, going in and coming out, praying and committing, daily. Most of these occasions are very familiar. The door opens easily most often, the journey is well-known. Now and again the door may need a push, and it may open on to a new room or a new path; on those occasions perhaps passing through it comes as a mild surprise.

And now and again you push the door, or you respond to a

knock on the door, and stepping through it you are transformed, and the view changes radically as you come in or go out. Such a moment could be your religious conversion, if you are religious. Or (a similar experience) you give yourself to another person in marriage or partnership, so that in the rooms and on the paths the presence of your beloved is all-pervasive, sometimes faint and sometimes strong, but always there. Or you step through at another hinge-moment in your life, perhaps the moment of committing to your life's work, or the moment of surrendering that commitment. Some of these key moments may be long-planned, and others will come as a big surprise.

In 2022, I experienced one of these once-in-a-lifetime moments when I retired from so-called active Christian ministry, and from my work as Bishop of Liverpool. Another came not long afterwards, as I shall relate.

Anyway, there is the picture – of the place in your spirit that leads to your inner being in one direction, and to your involvement in the world in the other; the door of your life that opens into rooms, or out upon paths, offering decisions for you to make, decisions that shape you.

And imagining this, you might imagine more; imagine for example that the rooms link together, and that the paths diverge – imagine a great diversity on each side of the door, a rich choice laid out for you whenever you step through.

Remembering Lewis, then, and using this image of the door in particular in the context of Christian faith, you may wish to imagine spirituality and action as a twofold seeking; seeking God as you approach this inward and outward journey, seeking God to learn how to make the choices involved, how to become who you are meant to be, how you are to see God where God is.

You may identify a room within, perhaps a busy room echoing with the words of the like-minded, perhaps a quiet and empty room. You may approach the choice of paths outside, some bustling and walled and well-paved paths, leading perhaps to and from churches; some more open, to the wider common life of human beings; some again narrow and overgrown and still and winding and lonely.

These journeys, the inward and the outward journeys, have given rise to much rich thinking in the long history of the Christian people. Earlier in this book I spoke of the introduction of Liverpool's

Rule of Life, a simple instrument in which we attempted to catch the twofold movement in and out, and to point all our people to the resources that all this thinking has shaped and offered. We did so as best we could, using words to match people's capacity and readiness to hear, and trying to speak according to the traditions in which this thinking came to them, some traditions more helpful for some than for others no doubt.

For all of us at some point, and for some of us all the time, the task has been to check first that the advice about rooms and paths is sound, and then to follow it religiously. Doing so leads you within to those rooms that are well decorated and very brightly lit, and leads you outside to those paths that are clearly signposted 'Christian' and that have been protected with walls – well-lit rooms and closely-walled paths, all kept in very good repair.

But there is always the possibility that you will find other rooms and other paths – small and half-hidden rooms, quieter and more unobtrusive paths. And for some of us it is these paths and these rooms that seem to speak most clearly of God.

Over forty-five years ago I read a book by John Drury, *The Pot and the Knife*. In its foreword he points to ' … some more personal debts. To the clergyman at a King's Lynn lecture course who told me that God was both more transcendent and more immanent than is generally supposed (he has since become a social worker).'[18] Drury's book is excellent. In its treatment of images and narratives (what he calls symbols and myths) it prefigures this present one, but with a good deal more subtlety and depth.[19] But it is that brief acknowledgement which has stayed with me for all these years, and which has been for me a compass in the paths I choose and the ways I walk.

God is both more transcendent and more immanent than is generally supposed. Jesus is both fully human and fully divine; not a bit of both, and not superhuman either. The door can open into a room and the room is empty. The door can open onto a path and the path leads you to the public world, bypassing the paved and well-lit paths to the church. In these recent years I have come to believe more and more that for me God is to be found in the desert and in the public place, and that it is deceptively easy, and mistaken, to look for God in some middle place, some self-consciously religious place, less transcendent and less immanent, instead a bit of both, availably supernatural, reliably available, unquestionably predictable, a middle place like a pocket where meaning and God can be tucked away and preserved.

I have not always acted on this sense of emptiness and unvarnished public life, mystique and politique. For some years I was an enthusiastically charismatic Christian; in other years I relished the glory of Cathedral worship and I was nourished by it. In my professional ministry I focused on the existence, sometimes on the survival, of the church as an institution, the brightly lit inner room and the well-walled path. I do not regret those years, and I do not regret inhabiting the rooms and walking the paths they indicate, wide and well-populated as they are.

But as I have grown older and as life has fallen in on me, I have come to find these rooms and roads too smooth. The lights that illuminate them have become too bright for me. I have turned (or sometimes returned) to less well-travelled paths, paths further from the bustle and closer to the edge of the wood, where the light is dimmer. For me these have been lonelier and more bracing paths which carry the clean odour of unvarnished reality, and along which I have found Jesus once again.

I do not say all this to offer a model for you. The journey I describe is not an inevitable journey, and indeed it can be a painful and unenviable one. To go within there may lead you to rooms that are visited less often and may be neglected, containing strange fixtures which may or may not be treasure. To go outside there may lead you to quiet and overgrown paths that have meandered out of the way altogether, petering out in fields or in deserts around the wood without the shade of the walls to sustain them, so that you find after all no abiding city there.

But nor do I say all this to put you off. Despite these risks, perhaps you will be enriched by the echoes of silence, or by strange flowers that you have never seen before, or not seen for ages. Perhaps you will discover or remember, and in either case you may be, yes, enriched.

So there it is; a wide and significant choice of rooms in your house and paths from your door, including the quieter places made and trodden by believers who have opened doors into quieter rooms over the years, rooms and paths left as gifts for those who come after, if they choose to enter or to walk them.

And it seems to me that to be a thinking Christian is to know the way into many rooms and onto many paths, to curate or treasure these, to abide in them and to walk them; and this is discipleship as I see it. Passing through the big door of retirement I turned a corner and saw some of the rooms and paths I had trodden before, when perhaps as a younger man I was freer to explore. I returned to these places and these paths, through their own smaller doors, with a sense of relief. Because the noise in the brighter rooms and along the walled paths was becoming too shrill and tiring, as people fought over the placing of the walls and the colour of the rooms, neglecting the silence within and the world outside. And it was time to dial down.

In the early days of my retirement I welcomed the space in these quieter rooms and the view from these quieter paths, not uncritically, but with gladness, nonetheless. I reconnected with my younger self, and God led me back to places I knew before and had forgotten. And all this was before the crisis of our lives came, as if God were preparing me indeed to face the altitude, the cold rooms and desert paths, reminding me of the resources of my whole life and not just of my priestly or episcopal life.

In the first lines of his *Divine Comedy*, Dante has something of the same sense: 'Midway upon the road of our life I found myself within a dark wood, for the right way had been missed.'[20] Sometimes, as for Dante, people feel bad, finding their paths smudged or blurred, freshly unclear in the middle of the wood, and they have to set out carefully along new paths, or perhaps to walk on virgin ground with no path at all for a few steps or a few yards or a few miles. Sometimes, as for Dante, from time to time the road seems to have run out.

This sense of walking along strange and unfolding paths has marked my own life's journey. In the busy-ness of my ministerial life, the strangeness of the unfolding path was itself blurred by the smudging effect of day-to-day routines and meetings and decisions and choices. Now in my retirement the sense of strangeness is very strong once again.

In Liverpool we said that we were called by God and sent by God; called on the inner journey to pray and read and learn, sent on the outer journey to tell and serve and give. Liverpool's Rule of Life was by no means unique – indeed I remember the sense of excitement when at a meeting of bishops (one of those rare meetings when we spoke to one another of what we were actually doing as bishops) it emerged that many of us were exploring in one way or another a rule, a discipline of the Spirit to offer our Dioceses.

All of us were speaking of rooms in the heart; all of us were speaking of paths through the world. In Liverpool we tried not to build walls around our preferred paths. We encouraged people to continue the walk along the paths that God had shown them, and yet not to pitch camp on any path or to engage in a permanent picnic there, still less to block the way for others coming behind. We recognised that people who were sent on the same path of action may have been called on different paths of reflection, and vice versa. And we celebrated this as an aspect of the limitless divine diversity.

The inner journey leads through the door that the Bible tells us to close behind us,[21] the door into the secret room where the nourishment of God is to be found. For myself I have found that nourishment in glory and ecstasy, yes; but even more fully in silence and in emptiness.

The outer journey leads through that same door. If you pass through it, it will lead you directly and without a private garden into the public space where some people flourish and others suffer, and where decisions must be made about where you stand and who you call your friends and what you do about that.

So you open the door and choose the room and the path. The rooms and paths you choose have been furnished and trodden before, but you must choose them for yourself. All this is one way of looking at the following of Christ, built on scriptural imagery and personal imagination.

As a drama undergraduate in the 1970s I was immersed in the thinking of Bertolt Brecht, who treasured a way of affecting the audience in the theatre which in German he called the 'Verfremdungseffekt'. Usually in English this is translated 'the alienation effect', but this can get people tangled in ideas of social alienation, not least because Brecht was a Marxist. But the German word *verfremden* means to make strange. Brecht's own explanation of the 'V-effect' was straightforwardly practical: 'The V-effect consists of turning the object of which one is to be made aware ... from something ordinary, familiar, immediately accessible, into something peculiar, striking and unexpected.'

Let's try out this V-effect, then, on an image for the life of faith. One unexpected view does not appear in a Christian book, but in

The New Buddhism, a committed and excellent reflection by David Brazier.[22] His Buddhist language and images can offer 'something peculiar, striking and unexpected', can offer a distancing. In this case it's a distance which has helped me to see my own tradition more clearly.

In that book Brazier writes to commend an uncluttered, personally disciplined, socially engaged Buddhism. He uses images to do this – images drawn from his own tradition in ways that have illuminated my own for me. Here's one: the image of the river or the stream.

> ... the kind of enlightenment taught by Shakyamuni Buddha was basically a two-step process. People who had taken the first step were called sotapanna. A sota is a stream or torrent, like the one the Buddha himself had to cross. Panna means to go down into it. A sotapanna is therefore a stream enterer.'[23]

In Brazier's world to be a stream-enterer is to be one who has begun the path of discipleship. The image is drawn from Buddhism, yet it has value for me as a Christian, opening as it does a range of echoes and reflections from my own experience. To take a concept (in this case in Pali or Sanskrit), and to unfold the image within it, is to teach in the way the Lord Jesus taught, the way I also have hoped to teach. And the strange image can then become my own, too.

The image is new to me; not part of my own tradition, and yet it's full of potential for enriching the way I go myself. Just one example: having entered the stream, it is not sufficient to face downstream and to go with the flow. On the contrary the task is to take one's stand in the face of the current, and to push upstream. Archbishop Desmond Tutu enriched this metaphor with his own image of seeing people in a stream, flowing by, in deep distress. The task, said Tutu, was not only to pull people out but to travel upstream so as to discover who was pushing them in.

I'll let the stream flow away now; it's tangential to the theme of these fragments. But it encourages me further to believe that images can reach beyond concepts, and that doors and rooms and paths, too, may have a relevance even beyond the Christian family. It should indeed be so if our humanity opens the way to God, as Jesus' did.

It is a commonplace, or perhaps just a joke, that every preacher has only one sermon in her or him. I don't believe that this is so, but if you're a preacher and you find a central image that communicates, treasure it and use it and repeat it. In my time in Liverpool I tried to do this with the image of the table, and here I am, trying to do the same with the image of the door. I don't apologise for the measure of repetition that this way of working demands.

Writing of the theatre, Peter Brook said this:

> When emotion and argument are harnessed to a wish from the audience to see more clearly into itself – then something in the mind burns. The event scorches on to the memory an outline, a taste, a trace, a smell – a picture. It is the play's central image that remains, its silhouette, and if the elements are rightly blended this silhouette will be its meaning, this shape will be the essence of what it has to say.[24]

Doors and rooms and paths have become such a picture for me, as I have brooded on them over the past three or so years. I hope that you, reading this, will have your own picture or pictures, too, as something in your own mind has burned. Your picture will have been inspired by your attention to scripture and by all you know of God through the teaching and life of the Church. It will have been nurtured in your own imagination and reflection, and it will have been tempered and honed in conversation with others. Like Jesus' own stories, it will transcend argumentative abstraction by referring to concrete and simple things, freighting them with the love and truth of God as the imagination of your listeners is ignited in its turn by what you say and share.

In his inaugural remarks when he was introduced as Archbishop of Canterbury in 2002, Rowan Williams ended by saying: '…if there is one thing I long for above all else is that the years to come will see Christianity in this country able to capture the imagination of our culture, to draw the strongest energies of our thinking and feeling into the exploration of what our creeds put before us.'[25] Almost a quarter of a century later, having witnessed and shared in our ceaseless, wearying internal Christian bickerings and chatterings, that is my longing too.

All glorious within

'To put it boldly, contemplation is the only ultimate answer to the unreal and insane world that our financial systems and our advertising culture and our chaotic and unexamined emotions encourage us to inhabit. To learn contemplative practice is to learn what we need so as to live truthfully and honestly and lovingly. It is a deeply revolutionary matter.'
(Rowan Williams)

'The climate in which monastic prayer flourishes is that of the desert, where the comfort of man is absent, where the secure routines of man's city offer no support, and where prayer must be sustained by God in the purity of faith.'
(Thomas Merton)

When I was Bishop of Hertford, in St Albans Diocese, I connected with a priest of the Diocese who was dying. I would visit this man in his home from time to time, to talk and listen and pray with him. He was not in much pain, but he was fading. I treasured these conversations in the midst of my work as a bishop, because the only thing he wanted to talk about was God. God, and not the church and its latest doings. This man had travelled the road of his own mortality into a region where the doings of the church were not important to him anymore. He had not lost his commitment; he had not regretted his ministry of many years; but at the end of his life he was focusing on the thing that mattered most to him. 'God is the interesting thing about religion', Evelyn Underhill wrote to the Archbishop of Canterbury in 1931, 'and people are hungry for God'. It was so for this man, and it is increasingly so for me.

'The King's daughter is all glorious within', says the Psalm, 'her clothing is of wrought gold. She shall be brought unto the King in raiment of needle-work'. And in the letter to Titus: 'The grace of God has dawned upon the world with healing for all humankind'. It was on subjects like this that the priest in St Albans was meditating, and it is on subjects like this that we are all ultimately called to reflect, if only we can tear our eyes away from the doings of the churches, and in particular from expatiating endlessly on the falling-short of the churches from the beauty of the Lord.

The inner journey of prayer is a road less travelled, but the Church is a big community and many millions of people are serious about it. To close the door and enter the secret place is by definition a private matter, at least at first. But in that secret place the Christian is never alone. Indeed it can become a pretty crowded place, but at its most empty the presence of God is guaranteed, guaranteed that is for those who have made the commitment of faith.

On 29 June 1980 I was ordained priest in Newcastle Cathedral. On 7 August 1980, then the Feast of the Holy Name in their calendar, I was admitted as a priest-associate of the Sisters of the Love of God (SLG), a contemplative Anglican community whose roots are in the Carmelite tradition and whose mother house is in Oxford. I have been one ever since.

My own life has been a disjointed one, but I have known what I wanted. I asked to become a formal associate of SLG because I saw in this community of women an authenticity of spirituality that I wanted to share. When I visited them as a student, when I saw them sitting in silence, when I shared their meals in silence, as I spoke to them on the rare occasions when this was possible, I felt the truth of their lives, these unobtrusive and serious women. Of course they knew how to smile and laugh and celebrate; but fundamentally they had chosen to sacrifice most of the options of their lives so as to go about a serious business. I wanted to associate with this, because I saw and valued the lived experience of these women whose lives were given to prayer in the desert, to the inner room and the closed door.

At some point in any Christian life the opportunity comes to pass through the door that swings between the inner and the outer world, so as to enter the quiet room and to close the door. I was drawn in this direction before my ordination, as a theological student, when I visited SLG, firstly in that mother house in Oxford and then in what was a more experimental community of sisters called primarily to be solitaries, at Bede House near Staplehurst in Kent. In those years I came to know the remarkable guiding eminence of the place, Mother Mary Clare, whose reflections on the life of prayer have sustained so many people[26]. She placed the desert journey of faith in the familiar context of the Gospel when she wrote: 'God draws us not merely into the dark cloud, but into the tremendous stillness of the height of Calvary, and through Calvary to the dawn of the new day.'

Mother Mary Clare established the spirit of her community in partnership with a man called Gilbert Shaw. He was one of those eccentric, upper-class Anglo-Catholics[27] whose authenticity of faith burned away a good deal of cultural lace (though he is reputed to be one of the inspirations for Father Chantry-Pigg in Rose Macaulay's sublime novel *The Towers of Trebizond*). Fr Gilbert's ministry involved a great deal of time spent with the poor, and in prayer with and for the spiritually oppressed ('demonised').[28] Along with this he worked for years in the East End of London, fighting especially for justice on behalf of the tenants of private landlords, who were regularly gouged and evicted and oppressed. Not everyone fought on their behalf. As one of the secular leaders of that community commented, 'the high church Anglicans and the Communists were the only active people in the East End'.[29] For Gilbert Shaw the door into the quiet room also led to the public square and the struggle for justice.

You see here a combination of a lively awareness of spiritual conflict, a commitment to corporate and political struggle, and a regular recourse to the quiet and empty room within. It is not a common combination, but it is not vanishingly rare. It is a combination that recurs in the life of the churches. I bring to mind for example the names of Dan Berrigan, Dorothy Day, John Halsey, Gilbert Shaw, Joan Chittister, Roland Walls, Bill Kirkpatrick, Ken Leech, together with more unlikely allies about whom I could have written more; many Friends who follow the Quaker way, and from the Pentecostal/Charismatic world John Wimber and Brent Rue. And among those who from a cloistered life inspired this same combination you will find Thomas Merton, and the Trappist martyrs of Tibhirine, and Mother Mary Clare.

I remember visiting Mary Clare once in her room in the convent, and her telling a story of that handful of sisters of her community who felt themselves called to the hermit life. 'Off they go,' she said, 'and they come back full of the lovely experiences of nature and beauty and so on: "Oh Mother," they say, "it's all so sublime". I say, "Yes, yes". Then one day they come in and sit down, all dispirited, and they say to me, "Oh Mother, I'm so bored!" And I say "Good. Now you can begin".'

The SLG ethos was inspired by the Carmelite saints, and the Carmelite way is not an easy one. 'What does it matter if the mind seems to be vacant and stupid? The heart is still, imperceptibly, awake to God'.[30] And then you can begin – begin what? Begin the journey of selflessness and of an intention to be one with the invisible Christ, even in His own uncertainty and suffering; begin in the slightest way to understand what the apostle meant when he wrote: 'I am now rejoicing in my sufferings for your sake, and in my flesh I am completing what is lacking in Christ's afflictions for the sake of his body, that is, the church.'[31]

I hope this does not sound highfalutin and exalted. It is not so. The finest English interpreter of the Carmelite way in my time has been Ruth Burrows, a sister of the Roman Catholic Carmel at Quidenham in Norfolk. Here she is on the life of faith:

> As it is, we are set over a gold mine, a shovel is put in our hands, we are given the strength to dig and the absolute assurance that if we do so we shall find ... What happens? Some of us at any rate set to work and dig but what we find is not at all what we expected. We expected a glistening nugget and instead all we have in our weary hands is an ugly, shapeless lump of metal. 'It is gold, pure gold,' we are told. But it doesn't look like gold, it doesn't feel like gold. You say you believe in Jesus. He told you that if you dug you would find the treasure. Where is your faith?'[32]

And here she is again, on how it feels to sit in that inner room:

> What is the essence of your grief, when all is said and done? Isn't it two things; a sense that you lack God, call it absence, call it abandonment, and at the same time a devastating awareness of your own wretchedness? Oh, I know, not in the least like what

John of the Cross writes about, that is what you are hastening to tell me, nothing grandiose like that, just drab petty meanness and utter ungodliness. Yes, but that is what he is talking about.[33]

This way of life will summon those who are called to it. As the writer of the Cloud of Unknowing is at pains to stress, it is not a way of life that will bless you unless you are indeed called.[34] My own journey has been uninspiring – halting, distracted, often unwilling to face the cost of oblation. And despite all this, the exercise of the believing will in the silence of prayer, in the real presence of the absent and invisible God, has been for me what goes on when I enter my inner room and close the door, as Jesus asked me to do.[35] It can bring about a stepping out in faith, a moment of inchoate trust in God, which has the same character irrespective of the levels of fervour and tradition and emotional swirlings or the lack of them, everything caught by the baleful word 'churchmanship'. It is the unglamorous and usually dry determination to accept that the lump of ugly metal in my weary hand is indeed my promised gift.

As a way of being a Christian, this is many miles away from the public ecstasies and boosterish cheerinesses with which the inner life is frequently sold to unbelievers, the instrumental salesmanship which runs 'statistics show that people with a religious faith have fewer breakdowns/fewer ulcers/longer life/happier days than those without' and the like.

As a poor follower in this way I want to witness to those who have travelled far upon it; to witness to those who close the inner door and enter the desert. Their own witness is remarkably consistent, both in the description of experience (or the lack of it) in the inner room itself, and in the way that those who dwell in that room are also led to identify with the poor, and with the struggle for justice. One example: René Voillaume, the Catholic priest who founded the Little Brothers of Jesus, placed the prayer of the desert in the context of the cross of Christ, calling it 'The Prayer of the Poor' and writing:

> God (we must be convinced of this by now) can only come to meet us in the measure in which our love is real; and we can only find the realness of love on the road of pure faith; and the road of pure faith passes through that dark region where reason

and feelings are reduced to their true dimensions, and 'put in their place.' Now, such a reduction, such a 'stripping down,' is required not only by the very nature of purification, but also by the Lord's usual manner of acting since he cannot come near us without our being touched by the fire of his agony and his cross.[36]

Several years before the Little Brothers were founded, their guiding spirit died alone in the desert – this time the literal desert of southern Algeria. The story of Charles de Foucauld has been told many times, and I shall not repeat it here.[37] But as I reflect on the King's daughter, all glorious within, I do want to share another story with you, the story of a prayer of Charles de Foucauld, and the way that prayer was given to me.

Later in this book,[38] I tell two or three stories of Roland Walls, an extraordinary priest and religious explorer, who left the possibility of a 'career' in the Church in order to be immersed in a small village in Midlothian, there to pray, to teach, to laugh and to suffer for over forty years, and in the end to witness the twilight of his community, as its three original members aged and faced the fact that the community would die with them, beginning with Roland himself.

His community, the Community of the Transfiguration, was located in Roslin, a small village mostly notable today for Rosslyn chapel, a place made famous or infamous by Dan Brown in his novel *The Da Vinci Code*. And the three members of the community who stayed with it their lives long were Roland, Patty Burgess and a man called John Halsey.

As Bishop of Hertford I would visit from time to time the parishes of Great and Little Gaddesden, in a part of south Hertfordshire whose life was bound up with the Halsey family, as it has been since before the dissolution of the monasteries by Henry VIII in the mid-sixteenth century.[39] In a parallel universe I might have met John Halsey in that context, since he was a member of that family, and his natural and expected path in life might have been to play his part in the management of the estate, or if he was ordained perhaps to have been the vicar of those churches. But, as it is, I met him in a cold, damp wooden hut with a tin roof in Midlothian, the converted miners' welfare building in Roslin which was the home of the Community of the Transfiguration.

I met him there because John Halsey chose to follow Christ in a different way from his forbears. Part of his training for ministry had been in Sheffield, in a group of people who were drawn together by Roland Walls and immersed in working-class life and employment alongside study and prayer. It was an experiment in creative ministry which, like too many others, died away without gaining much purchase on the mainstream traditions of formation.

And when subsequently Roland Walls founded the Community of the Transfiguration, it was with John Halsey that he did so.[40] And Brother John, living in a small hut in the garden of the old miners' welfare, rising before dawn for an hour's silent prayer each day, went on then to work for his living, originally as a miner underground, and then for many years as a polisher in the paint shop of a garage (a role he combined with that of a union official in the garage, negotiating and advocating on behalf of his colleagues with the management of the place). He was doing this job when I visited the Roslin community for a retreat, sometime in the early 80s, when I was working as a University Chaplain in London.

Elsewhere, I write of the purifying and positive impact on me of Don Cupitt's non-realist critique of modern Christian faith. It is compelling, and if a theologically honest person doesn't at least feel the force of it I wonder whether they have been thinking enough. But for me it is balanced, and counterbalanced and overmatched, by an irreducible clinging to the mystery of the real God – summed up perhaps in the image in my mind of some books in Greek in one of the rooms at Roslin.

Sometimes you can tell a book by its cover. The books in that room were damp, and many of them were covered in a thin layer of mould. Among them the mouldy volumes of the early church writers spoke of lives lived long ago, and lived in a certain way, in faithfulness to the Jesus-event and to the way that was interpreted in the early centuries of the Church.

The existence of those books in that place spoke of a valuing of human intelligence such that the Patristic languages are worth learning, understanding and discussing. And it spoke of a lifestyle such that the poor are the infinite priority; a lifestyle of poverty, not 'for the poor' but with the poor indeed, not in a warm library but in a cold and damp and uncomfortable room. It spoke of an offering of life to the silence of prayer and the struggle of the poor, held together in an extraordinary unity.

The Roslin community eschewed success, and was intensely relaxed about its smallness and its fragility, because it saw itself as a sign rather than a movement. More than the many and real glories of Christianity, it is to the sign in Roslin that I cling in my retirement, after a lifetime attempting to serve God and the world and falling short.

Many years ago, as a curate, I remember reading in Thomas Merton's *Way of the Desert* the story of the monk Serapion, who sold his copy of the Gospels with the words, 'I have sold the book that told me to sell everything I have and give the money to the poor'. After I read that I lifted my eyes to look at the nineteen Bibles on my shelves, and I felt the force of that sign as Serapion lived it, just as later I felt the force of the sign lived at Roslin. It's a sign that points beyond philosophy, though part of its road involves the most minute scrutiny of human texts. But it points to the living God who is perceived in emptiness and silence and hard manual labour, not in glory and power and luxury. It is that living God whom I seek to worship and to serve still.

The community had an open door, and if you went there on retreat you were welcome, but no more welcome than the travellers and people of the road with whom you shared meals and among whom you had a bed in the dormitory. My mother worked as a home-help supervisor, and after her round of visits from day to day she would climb fully clothed into the bath and shake her clothes out to check if she had picked up fleas from the home-help clients' homes. At the end of my days in Roslin I would need to do the same; the only retreat house in my experience where that was a necessary step.

Alongside walks with Roland, which were powerfully reminiscent of the stories of the desert fathers of the early church,[41] I was also able to talk to Brother John about his work, and his prayer, and his life. As a parting gift for me he wrote, on a carefully torn scrap of paper, the Prayer of Abandonment of Charles de Foucauld, which the Community prayed daily. I treasure that scrap of paper above any other Christian document I own, certainly more than my certificates of ordination, or the letters patent of the monarch on my appointment as a bishop, or my writ of summons to the House of Lords. I treasure it for the sake of the life I was shown at Roslin, by Roland Walls certainly but perhaps even more clearly by John Halsey; a life of oblation and abandonment, a life combining the silence of the quiet room with the noise of the paint-shop and of the union meeting; a full and a Christian life, utterly weak and defeated in the eyes of the world, all glorious within:

> Father
> I abandon myself into your hands
> Do with me what you will
> Whatever you do, I will thank you
> Let only your will be done in me
> As in all your creatures
> And I'll ask nothing else, my Lord
> Into your hands I commit my spirit
> I give it to you with all the love of my heart
> For I love you, Lord, and so need to give myself
> To abandon myself into your hands
> With a trust beyond all measure
> Because you are my Father.

The crowded threshold

*Then he went home, and the crowd came together
again, so that they could not even eat.*
(Mark 3:20)

*The desert is squeezed in the tube-train next to you,
The desert is in the heart of your brother.*
(T. S. Eliot, 'The Rock')

*Manicurist: 'Do you want your nails long or short?'
Otis B. Driftwood: 'You better make them short, it's
getting kind of crowded in here!'*
(Marx Brothers, A Night at the Opera)

In one of the most famous scenes in film comedy 'three stowaways have to hide out in a small cabin on board a luxury liner while a parade of people walk in, asking to either use the cabin, or to perform their regular duties. Crammed into this little space at the end of the scene are Driftwood, Fiorello, Tomasso, Ricardo, two cleaning ladies who make up the bed, a manicurist, a ship's engineer and his large assistant, a young woman passenger using the phone to call her Aunt Minnie, a maid (Maid: "I come to mop up." Driftwood: "You'll have to start on the ceiling.") and four waiters with trays of hard-boiled eggs. (Driftwood: "Tell Aunt Minnie to send up a bigger room.") All of the foregoing tumble out into the hallway when Mrs. Claypool opens the door.'[42]

It may seem that this Marx Brothers scene of comic overcrowding has little to do with the quiet of the desert. But I am convinced that the two images, the empty room and the crowded threshold, are intimately linked by and through the ministry of Jesus, and that as disciples we are called to enable both, so that God's grace may operate through both.

Péguy was wrong to say that everything begins in mysticism and ends in politics. Sometimes the social choices you make can then open the door to authentic prayer. In my own life I have known the spiritually transforming power of action in the world, and of allowing the friends of Jesus to enter the space in the heart.

This connection needs to be reinforced in these days. The voices of 'Christian nationalism' are growing across the world, as is the attempt to baptise self-interest first, then to prefer those lovely people who are like me, and certainly to exclude the unwashed, the unlike and the unlovely in the name of a God of purity. It will not wash. Precisely the excluded poor will be admitted if we respond to the knock on the door, the knock of Jesus Christ who stands among the unloved and calls them his friends, and who cannot be received without them.

Similarly the growth of secular mindfulness, usually designed to improve performance and effectiveness in the service of capital, is a sign of the detachment of our society from the messy God who associates with the poor, and who cannot be welcomed without them.

In Norman Jewison's 1975 film *Rollerball* the hero Jonathan E is invited to visit the corporate villain, the executive Mr Bartholomew (beautifully played incidentally by John Houseman) in his office, a place of calm and stillness with glass rods hanging and quiet music, and the first thing Bartholomew says to him is 'Come in, Jonathan. Keep silence with me for a minute, won't you?' – and they sit in meditation, or at least Bartholomew does.

I often recall that scene when I read of the application of mindfulness in the commercial world. 'Come in, Jonathan. Keep silence with me for a minute, won't you?' – keep silence with me before I silence you, and tell you what to do, and reduce you to your place in my corporate world. Breathe in with me, so that your lungs are too full for action. False peace, where there is no peace. Talk of love in a bubble of likeness, closed to the diverse world that God has given us to love in fact.

By contrast, across the ages Christian disciples have learned to treasure the desert place and to treasure the crowded room, as God has led and shaped them. People learn these lessons in different places. I learned mine in the school of nonviolent direct action, outside the gates of RAF and USAF bases in the 1980s, as a member of Christian CND, sitting in the snow beside Quakers and Dominicans and Buddhists and pagans and atheists. I learned on the soup run in central London, as a University Chaplain, alongside students of all kinds who had joined the student society 'Comac' (Community Action), so that with all our diverse motivations we could be in solidarity with those who were in need, and the question 'deserving or undeserving?' was not a question that mattered, not a question for us to answer.

This twofold movement can easily be domesticated. Lady Bountiful is alive and well in the twenty-first century. In his *Liberating God*, Peter Selby says: 'there seems to me to be some way in which those who have received some pastoral and spiritual formation incline to involvement in some political issues rather than others (if they involve themselves in any). The ones we choose seem to be those which are most clearly universal and which also engage us most at the level of our interior lives. They seem to involve us less in the partial and ambiguous solidarity that most often characterise political activity.'[43]

To be rightly open to the crowds is to be open to human need in all its unmanageable and invasive messiness. Al Barrett and Ruth Harley write compellingly of this in their excellent *Being Interrupted*.[44] This should not lead to despair. As I used to say to my colleagues in parochial ministry, even in a small community the sum of human need is for all practical purposes infinite. So there is no reason to feel depressed or defeated if our resources cannot match the need. As John Wimber used to say (a phrase I shall revisit later in this book): 'It's not our job to get God off the hook.' If all we can offer is a token response, what should our token be? To whom should we pay attention?

In all this there are choices to make, and surprises to be encountered. In each of our lives we will have experienced the moment when the meeting of need comes as a surprise. It would be lovely to feel that we can take an overview of the infinity of need, and always make a good choice as to what we will offer as help, and to whom. But that can only be achieved if we shut the door to those who come accidentally to it.

As a parish priest, in Buckinghamshire and in Hampshire, I was frequently interrupted in my daily work and life by the knock on the door and the request, or more often the demand, for a cup of tea and a snack. Parochial clergy reading this will know what I mean. One of our more regular visitors was highly selective in his approval of what was offered, with the discriminating palate of a restaurant critic. 'Haven't you got any ham?' he would say querulously, on being presented with a cheese sandwich. Or, 'What, no tomatoes again?' We had to admit that there were none.

To make room for human need should issue in political choices. As a serving bishop at election time I once posted a thought on social media, asking that people might use this question as a yardstick for voting: 'How can my vote help and serve the poorest of the poor?' It's a question that can genuinely be answered positively across a large section of the spectrum of political choice. But that didn't stop people from accusing me of being a woke lefty bishop. They may well have been right; but not because I posted that particular message. If Jesus is accompanied into your heart by the people he served in his earthly ministry, and by the equivalent of those people today, then political decision will be sharpened and prayer made more valid.

From many traditions comes the testimony that the crowded threshold and the empty room within are intimately linked. In his book *The Jesus Prayer*, Simon Barrington-Ward recalls this story of the Staretz Silouan. Silouan was a contemplative monk, yet also a person who was approached by many for intercessory prayer. Recalling one young family living in poverty and great need, Silouan said this:

> In the beginning I prayed with tears of compassion for Nicholas, for his young wife and little child. But as I was praying the sense of the divine presence began to grow on me, and at a certain point it grew so powerful that I lost sight of Nicholas, his wife, his child, his needs and their village and I could be aware only of God. And I was drawn by the sense of the divine presence deeper and deeper until all of a sudden at the heart of this presence, I met the divine love holding Nicholas, his wife and his child. And it was with the love of God that I began to pray.[45]

At one time as a University chaplain I spent a season when for an hour a week I would sit in the company of a disturbed young student who had an almost disabling obsessive-compulsive disorder, which took the form of repeated hand-washing – his hands were raw and very painful to him. The offer of space must (I hope) have helped this man, since he chose to return for six or seven sessions before moving away from the college. We would sit in silence for the whole time. It seemed to me, since I did not know how to help or how to pray for this man, that each time we met I was descending into a dark pool and sitting there with no technique or even intention to help me, except the intention to ask God to heal him. Later in this book I try to explore the mystery at the heart of all faith, the mystery summed up in the repeated words of St John, 'No one has ever seen God'.[46] The time spent in prayer with and for this student was a reminder of this mystery, and of the helplessness of ministry which can nonetheless be used by God to heal.

For forty years it has seemed to me that this link between political and pastoral care for the hurting on the one hand, and contemplative stillness on the other, has a further dimension as we seek to live an authentic life. In 1986, in those University Chaplaincy years, I wrote about this in the journal of the Sisters of the Love of God, the 'Fairacres Chronicle'. I offer this older fragment here, since it seems to me that the twofold swinging of the door, and the need to connect with people at the crowded threshold, has things to say about who we are in God and who we will be in God in the end. I called the piece 'Moving among the Masks'.[47]

The man who got on the tube train saw the world slightly differently from most Londoners; just enough to make him speak very loudly and slowly, and to make him unusually friendly. He asked the way to Notting Hill Gate, in a strong cockney accent. No one really wanted to get involved, but eventually I spoke and we had a little conversation. As I got off the train I realised that I had been speaking as a cockney, although my natural accent veers between Yorkshire and BBC English. What had I been doing, or playing at? Reflecting on that question led me to these thoughts.

Before entering theological college, I studied drama and theatre arts. After I decided to become a priest, people who discovered that I was a drama graduate would say something like, 'Well, I'm sure your training as an actor will come in in useful in the church'. I suppose they meant that I would be able to make myself heard while preaching, or that I could run the parish dramatic society. But I was always a little disturbed by the implied suggestion that Ministry and acting were alike, because that went against something which I had come to believe – namely, that the Christian life was a matter of 'being yourself', of refusing to hide behind rules, I've becoming authentic.

I still believe that discipleship is about being authentic, but I have come to see that a disciple may also need to be an actor – though this flies in the face of popular notions about how to set about being real.

Spiritual writers, therapists, counsellors, rock musicians, novelists, all urge us powerfully to 'be honest', to 'be yourself'. The implication seems to be that all masks are false: to 'find yourself' means to find a bedrock personal identity underneath a whole series of masks and poses which we need to adopt to shield ourselves from pain. Those who have indeed 'found themselves' I thought to be free from the necessity to adopt roles or to 'put on an act'. They are the same people no matter where they go or with whom they speak. They always exercise the same blend of authority, humility, love, firmness, curiosity and helpfulness. In any situation, they remain who they really are.

Popular wisdom, nourished by versions of Freudian and post-Freudian psychology, has made this view of the true self common currency, and it is assumed by much contemporary psychotherapy and spirituality. But, adopted uncritically, it may seem to carry with it certain implications: first, that a 'false self' may be detected whenever people adapt their behaviour to fit in with others; secondly, that there is a natural 'true self' which has been buried by all this play acting, and which waits, dormant but alive, for the patient's process of self-examination and asceticism which will release and revive it.

I believe that this is a misunderstanding, and one that leads people to suffer a lot of heartache in their quest to find 'the real me' which will endure. Of course, it seems natural and right that Christian discipleship should involve monolithic honesty of this kind. The argument runs that since God is unchanging, and we are made in God's image and grow into God's likeness, we should assume and keep our true nature. For an actor to take on another character in the theatre has seemed deceitful and of the devil, the father of lies; the church has always suspected an element of hypocrisy in the theatre.

What I want to suggest is that moving in and out of roles, far from being a flight from authenticity, is in fact way of loving. The priest, actor, and sociologist Roger Grainger puts it clearly:

> You may be an extremely mild and gentle person, but you're looking for a nervous breakdown if you allow yourself to appear as such when you're faced with the task of bringing a playground full of children to order. On the other hand, if your job is a teacher involves counselling, you're not going to get any clients if you present yourself as a Company Sergeant Major ... the inability to recognise what you're doing when you change from one road to another is much more neurotic than the simple acceptance that you are not one but a whole range of characters.[48]

Put like that it seems an obvious matter; and yet deep inside we do not want to believe it. Some of the resistance is well-founded: it is indeed possible to flee love, by 'acting apart' in a whole range of inappropriate and deceptive ways. But it is also possible to adapt our behaviour in order to relax, help and care for the people we meet. In practice we do it all the time, perhaps with an uneasy sense that we are somehow playing false.

Was I, in the tube train, deceiving my new friend into thinking that I was from London? Or being patronising because I thought his accent quaint? Or was I presenting myself to him in the way which I subconsciously thought would be most helpful and least threatening? To meet and help people in a mature, appropriate way we need to be free of any lingering sense of bad faith in such a situation. It is the person who locks into one character, calling it 'the true self', who is refusing to grow, refusing to take other people seriously enough to want to be for them, and to change for them. We are well used to the need for people to adopt rules on public occasions – the priest, the judge or the diplomat. Why should the arena of our everyday experience be any different?

But there is a difference between acting and living, and it is that the actor has an off-stage life where she can 'be herself'. If all our lives are lifting roles, we must ask whether there is any 'true self' running through them all. Are we onion people with layers of roles masking emptiness? If any one of our 'selves' is just a character, then who are we?

To explore this I draw on the thinking of Thomas Merton who was deeply concerned with the matter of truth and falsehood in the self. By one stage Merton seems to have seen the whole purpose of monastic solitude and contemplation in terms of escape from the falsities engendered by social interaction: 'the creative and mysterious in a self must be delivered from the wasteful, hedonistic and destructive echo that seeks only to cover itself with disguises.' Here he seems close to the current ideas about authenticity to which I have been referring. But his perceptions were more subtle than that: 'it is possible to speak of the exterior self as a mask, but to do so is not necessarily to reprove it. The mask that each man wears may well be a disguise, not only for that man's inner self but for God, wandering as a pilgrim and exile in his own creation.'

For Merton, the true self is not a commodity to be possessed by those who work on themselves; and contemplation is not another form of self-improvement, a spiritual mud-pack to lift the dirt from the soul. Rather, in contemplation all that one can hope to do is to offer an arena within which the true self may emerge. Because in our deepest being we are at one with the spirit of God, the true self must be elusive, unpredictable, not to be grasped. 'The inner self is precisely that self which cannot be tricked or manipulated by anyone, not even the devil. The true self is like a very shy wild animal that never appears at all whenever an alien presence is at hand, and comes out only when all is peaceful, in silence, when one is untroubled and alone. The true self cannot be learned by anyone or anything, because it responds to no lure other than that of the divine freedom.'

The notion of the elusive true self is found in all the world's mature spiritual traditions, and Merton himself explored Taoist and Buddhist reflections on it. But in the context of my thinking here, it is most clearly to be seen in the Jewish existentialist Martin Buber, for whom, even more than for Merton, the dimension of relationship is paramount. Buber describes the quality of relationship with another, the 'I-Thou' relationship, in which there is no trace of manipulation or oppression. Thus it may only be entered by the true self. But precisely because this encounter is free from control, so also is its arrival free from control. 'The You encounters me by grace – it cannot be found by seeking'. Then, as suddenly as it came, the moment is gone: 'This … is the sublime melancholy of our lot, that every You must become an It in this world …'

Thus for Buber the true self, the deepest me, is not for me, but for Another. And therefore I cannot find myself alone, and I cannot hold onto myself. I cannot, because by that act of grasping, I would destroy the very air the true self breathes, the real but unknowable relationship with the invisible God.

This is most truly so in silent prayer. When I enter the dark pool of contemplation, when I reach out in blind trust for God, I am reaching out also for myself. Contemplation shows us that in a quite concrete sense we do not know who we are. It has to be enough for us to trust that God knows who we are, the God who is nearer to us than we are to ourselves.

And what then about role-play? There too we can be, not for ourselves, but for others. We are like the Invisible Man in Wells's story, who was only to be seen by his bandages. To the question, 'How do we know that these bandages do not also wrap distortions to the shape of ourselves?' we can only answer that they show the pattern of our true being to the extent that they are worn for love's sake; to the extent that we change the bandages to help the people we meet.

This insight, if it is true, liberates us from the illusory request for a true self in the human realm, and thus we are free to be flexible in our different human relationships. We never know when by grace we may meet another truly. In the meantime we are called to meet them in love. Surely St Paul grasped this clearly; for the same man who said, 'you have died, and your life is hid with Christ in God' and 'it is no longer I who live but Christ who lives in me', was also able to say, 'I have become all things to all people, that I might by all means save some'.[49] Was he not talking about these two movements of authentic Christian love, towards God and towards our neighbour?

With all that in mind, I believe that anyone's Christian identity is a reality for the end of time. In the book of Revelation we are told that in the end we will receive our name from the risen Christ, as we receive the news about who we really are: 'Let anyone who has an ear listen to what the Spirit is saying to the churches. To everyone who conquers I will give some of the hidden manna, and I will give a white stone, and on the white stone is written a new name that no one knows except the one who receives it.'[50]

The crowded threshold is a place of political decision, a place of profound intercession, a place of Christian soul-making and discovery. In my farewell sermon I said: '… the poor carpenter's threshold is not there to exclude any element. It is there to help you welcome and bless. It is not a step. It is like the ground around the bare tree on the bare hill where the poor carpenter died. No one is special at that threshold, and no one is excluded. All you need do is hold out your thin arms.'

Altitude

Thin air

*For the thing which I greatly feared is come upon me,
and that which I was afraid of is come unto me.
I was not in safety, neither had I rest, neither
was I quiet; yet trouble came.*
(Job 3:25, KJV)

*Kind people have said to me 'She is with God.' In
one sense that is most certain. She is, like God,
incomprehensible and unimaginable.*
(C. S. Lewis, *A Grief Observed*)

My wife Kate and I moved from Liverpool to our retirement home in Bath in April 2022. For four months we focused on settling in and establishing new rhythms of life. She had a number of good friends in the city, and her weekly routines were quickly established; they included lunch with those friends as well as two weekly commitments – a gentle ballet/exercise class for older women, 'Silver Swans', and a life drawing class. She had completed a novel in lockdown – intended as the first of four, a social comedy of 1950s village life[51] – and looked forward to writing the other three to complete the sequence. She explored the choirs of the city and made plans to join one of them. She worked each day on her stained glass, and received a commission from a hospice for a contemplative window for their chapel/quiet room. She fulfilled this commission, though the physical effort of cutting the glass tired her more than she expected. This was the first cloud on the horizon of her health.

Her tiredness was accompanied by some troubling symptoms: extremely high blood pressure; red flashes in her field of vision. It seemed too that her kidneys were functioning far less well than they should.

Still, at the end of August 2022 we prepared to travel to the United States where I had been offered a house-for-duty opportunity as an assisting bishop in the Diocese of Virginia for three months. We knew many friends in that Diocese, we were looking forward greatly to the opportunity. Kate's clothes were folded on her bed ready for packing, when she had an appointment with the GP to address her symptoms. At that meeting she was strongly advised not to travel.

We cancelled the trip and began a long course of tests and biopsies and consultations. A couple of months later, as the Autumn unfolded, Kate was provisionally diagnosed with multiple myeloma, an incurable cancer of the blood. Later this diagnosis was refined to a similar but much rarer cancer, the almost unpronounceable Waldenstrom's macroglobulinaemia, and she began a six-month course of chemotherapy in February 2023.

Throughout the chemo, in her own word, she felt poisoned. But we looked for improvement after the course of treatment ended. In Summer 2023 she contracted COVID and, immunosuppressed as she was, she tested positive for fifty days. We thought that this, and the after-effects of the chemotherapy, might explain why she was not recovering more quickly. But in Autumn 2023 she received a further diagnosis; amyloidosis of the kidneys and the heart, a rare complication for a rare cancer, where the build-up of proteins in the organs can produce progressive organ failure.

In particular the build-up of amyloid proteins in her heart was leading to heart failure, with its symptoms of steadily increasing fatigue and breathlessness. A new course of immunotherapy began.

These therapies depress the immune system and leave their patients very vulnerable to infection. In January 2024 Kate contracted a chest infection which led to neutropenic sepsis. For the next two months she was in and out of hospital, progressively weakening, unable to shake off a debilitating cough, plagued by diarrhoea and loss of appetite, deeply distressed that she was growing weaker and not stronger, despite the best efforts of our health team. Determined to face life, she persisted with the treatment. We explored a palliative care track, but she was clear that life was the way she would face, for as long as she could.

She died at home on 13 March 2024, in the arms of our elder daughter. She was 68 years old. We had been married for 48 years.

Hemingway writes of a bankrupt whose finances went wrong: 'Two ways: gradually, then suddenly.' So it was with Kate's declining health. Her death surprised us even though we were expecting it;

she died instantly of cardiac arrest. Death came into our home unrecognised, we who were facing life and expecting a longer goodbye. All our plans and hopes were overthrown gradually, then suddenly.

Many times each day I would say to her, 'Can I get you anything?' But what we both wanted for her was life, and I could not get her that, and nor could anyone else. Why? In the Psalms we read, '…because the payment for a human life is too great. What we could pay would never be enough to keep us from the grave, to let us live forever'.[52]

It is a well-trodden road, this way of degenerative illness and weakness and death. We walked the road with tens of thousands of others, a road beaten hard by the hundreds of millions who had walked it before us. It was in no way unusual; it was only unique.

Every morning through her illness I prayed these petitions for Kate: that she would be surrounded by God's golden, healing light, that there would be love at every step of the journey, that every one of our days would be a jewel to add to the jewel-box of days, and that the image in her own prayers – that Jesus was holding her close to the waterfall of healing life – would be increasingly true in her experience. I pray these petitions for her still, every day, though I do not know where she is. She is, like God, incomprehensible and unimaginable.

All her life Kate sought to be honest in her believing. Her Christian faith was constant, and so was her love for Jesus, who was experienced by her as a loving presence, a person she knew. But she was frankly sceptical about the afterlife, as she had been throughout her life.

We had many images of our experience. Here is one: as the journey of our retirement unfolded, and as her illness progressed, it was as if the pigments of our faith, the content of our understanding of God, became less brightly coloured as our journey progressed. They did not fade, but their colour departed.

Here is another image we used to crystallise our experience. As Kate's illness worsened we used to say that she was the mountaineer, and I was the sherpa. In the cancer ward we saw that this was the common pattern; for almost every mountaineer, a sherpa – a spouse or a child or a parent or a friend walking alongside as the mountain was climbed, until at the very summit each mountaineer had to press on, alone, unaccompanied.

And we noticed that for this sherpa and his mountaineer, as we climbed, the air grew thin. And in that thin air the doors of our lives continued to open, into new rooms or rooms long neglected, on to new paths and new involvements, even as the horizons drew in and it became hard to venture in or out at all.

Towards the end we had entered the high mountain zone, what those who climb high mountains call the death zone. And we found that we had no additional oxygen in our packs with which we might breathe yesterday's bottled oxygen – stale maybe, but nourishing for those who had it. But for us the liturgical and theological and companionable riches of the Church were in the valley below. We had not in any way risen above them; but we had left them behind, or they had left us behind. Kate and I breathed thin air together.

Another image; at these altitudes water boils at a lower temperature, and similarly the resources of the faith, the warm resources which had meant a lot to us in happier days, they boiled away now.

And yet we found that in thin air you can still breathe.

Samuel Johnson famously said, 'Depend upon it, sir, when a man knows he is to be hanged in a fortnight, it concentrates his mind wonderfully.' And John Macquarrie writes: 'What has to be taken into consideration if there is to be anything like a complete acceptance of the factical situation of human existence is death. For it is death more than anything else brings before us the radical finitude of our existence, and it is in the light of this that every possibility must be evaluated.'[53]

In the last months and weeks, when we spoke of these things and of God, Kate and I found agreement and hope in a very simple affirmation; that there was a mystery at the heart of the world and that this mystery was marked by love, pointed to love, was made of love. More than this we did not feel able to say. What will survive of us is love, we said, as Philip Larkin does in 'The Arundel Tomb'. We said it wholeheartedly – for us the instinct was true indeed – but we did not know what it meant, except that it was real, and it was a mystery of love.

In *The Foolishness of God*, John Austin Baker imagines the approach of many church people: 'namely, that there is Someone or Something behind it all, that Jesus was a good man, and that the betting on survival after death is evens'.[54] Keith Ward says much the same thing, in a higher register: 'at the centre of the human self there is some form of union or encounter with a reality which is felt to be both beyond the individual self and yet somehow at the very roots of one's personal being'.[55] You must not think that these writers are patronising, or talking down to, people with an unschooled faith. In the death zone Kate and I were not faithless, but these quiet words spoke to our condition, as the more fortissimo proclamations 'of the Gospel' did not and could not.

To use yet another image our faith had reduced, as a sauce reduces over the flame – perhaps gained in intensity, but certainly lost volume; reduced. And if there were words to it, they were simply these: there is a mystery, and that mystery is to do with love, and to that mystery we confide ourselves in death.

Now she is gone, and I sit here alone, in the house she shaped and we shared, weeping and writing these words. My grieving is sharp. It partakes of the common human experience, uniting me in the end with everyone who has ever loved and lost and mourned. But in my grief I seek theological as well as emotional resources, as I continue to gasp, to breathe thin air, as the door of my life opens at altitude. Mine is now a raw faith – not a 'pure' faith but raw, with nerve-ends exposed, not one which is cooked and basted and sealed in the ovens of an agreed and agreeable Christian apologetic.

What is the gospel for me and those like me? Where are the images of faith, where is the word of comfort? Not at any rate in the self-confident affirmations of Christian assurance. When my father was dying in the 1990s, I was attending a charismatic Christian summer festival with my family. The song of the moment contained these biblical lyrics: 'He's turned my mourning into dancing again.'[56] Each morning I would leave the festival to drive to his deathbed and to sit with him there as he faded. Each evening I would return to the campsite to hear that song being sung. It did not speak to me, or of me, or for me. What gospel spoke to me then? What gospel speaks to me now?

I have written at the head of this chapter those words of C. S. Lewis, from *A Grief Observed* – 'Kind people have said to me "She is with God." In one sense that is most certain. She is, like God, incomprehensible and unimaginable.'[57] In some of his other writings Lewis was well able to breathe the hearty air of a confident and problem-solving orthodoxy. But in the moment of grieving he was in the death zone. His tentative and honest and harsh words have helped me directly, as they have helped so many over the years. And yet in that moment he makes no affirmation.

Kate has died. She is, like God, incomprehensible and unimaginable. What does this say to me about God, or about the theological thoughts of the disciples after Jesus' death? What cobwebs of repeated and unthinking affirmation might it blow away in my mind, a mind full of the repeated reflexes of the working bishop called upon to 'say a few words', speaking repetitively, unreflectively, truly perhaps, but without attention to the air people must breathe? Where is the truth, here in the death zone?

In the sermon that begins this book I spoke of the inner room, and of the mystery of glory within, found most often for me in silence. And I said that Jesus knocks, and that he brings his friends with him into that space, with their own needs, holding out their thin arms.

I spoke of those thin arms because just before this sermon was preached in Liverpool Cathedral, Kate came to the lectern to share a well-known poem as her own farewell to the Diocese. When she did so, neither of us had any idea of the journey that lay ahead, the mountain we were to climb.

The poem she chose was 'The Coming' by R. S. Thomas, published in 1972 in his collection *H'm*. It portrays a world in bleak and uncompromising terms, a scorched land burned by a pitiless light. This harsh landscape is inhabited by 'many People'. They are marked by sadness and longing, but also by an inchoate hope; they hold out 'their thin arms' to a bare tree, as if they were living sculptures by Giacometti. The image of the tree recalls the Cross of course, but surely also the tree of Beckett's tragicomic portrait of despair, *Waiting for Godot* – a play which Kate both taught and directed in her years as a Head of Drama.

Holding out their thin arms the people hope (though hope is not a word that Thomas uses here). His image is of the universal hope 'for a vanished April to return', and the echoes of Easter cascade in the mind. Because, in contrast to Beckett's nihilistic vision, the final lines speak of 'the son', that is of Christ, who sees clearly and in its fulness the bleakness and pain of the human condition and yet who asks that he may 'go there', so as to stand with the people in their need, and in this way, knowing the cost, to bring salvation.

This poem and this image, in its brutal honesty and its breathtaking hope, had lived with Kate over many years. She wanted to share it with the Diocese as she made her own farewell.

And two years later, Kate held out her thin arms – and at the end they were very thin – and waited for a vanished April to return. She died in March, on one of the days which is always Lent, no matter the date of Easter; in Deep Lent. Now she is with God, incomprehensible, unimaginable. And I, grieving, need a theology that can make room for raw faith in thin air. I need people who have faced the hard questions, who have not fled the acid that life brings to faith if you let it, and who nonetheless have held something that lasts forever.

Yes, Jesus comes into our sorrow. Yes, Jesus is called by our sorrow to come. Yes, Jesus holds us. But the mode in which he holds us is beyond us; it is a mystery. I needed people who lived that mystery and who could commend it.

When as a theological student in the 1970s, I went on retreat to an Anglican Benedictine house, then at Nashdom Abbey. A monk came up to me and said, 'Oh, you're from Queen's. I thought all Queen's students carried a copy of *The Cloud of Unknowing* in their back pocket'. He laughed and so did I, though I was not sure what the joke was. But although the monk was (I think) joking, it is a pity that he was not correct. For those who need to live at this altitude, the Christian tradition has gifts to give. It is the tradition of *The Cloud of Unknowing* that offers help to mountaineers and sherpas, among other and equally unfashionable traditions.

This is a Christian thing, but other images can enrich it. In 'Arabian Sands' the great explorer Wilfrid Thesiger has this story to tell:

> I thought of that ruined castle in distant Syria which Lawrence had visited. The Arabs believed that it had been built by a prince of the border as a desert palace for his queen, and declared that its clay had been kneaded with the juice of flowers. Lawrence was taken by his guides from room to crumbling room. Sniffing like dogs they said, 'this is jasmine, this violet, this rose'; but at last one of them had called, 'Come and smell the very sweetest smell of all', and had led him to a gaping window where the empty wind of the desert went throbbing past. 'This', they told him, 'is the best: it has no taste'.[58]

Again, in a quiet churchyard in the Midlands is the grave of Nick Drake, the musician and poet of my youth who took his own life at the age of 26, in 1974, and in that way gained a sort of immortality, at least for now. Some years ago I visited that grave, and recently I have visited it again. Carved on the back of the headstone is a line from one of his songs: 'And now we rise, and we are everywhere'. It feels like that for me, as I reach out everywhere for my wife, and as I look for comfort from the Church, and its contemplatives, and its theologians.

Doors open, in to secret places and out onto public spaces. But the altitude at which you live changes over time, from the steamy, sea-level delights of a strong collective faith to the death zone, where standing with Jesus all you can do is cry out, My God, My God, why have you forsaken me? And for all I know it changes back again; the air thickens and an easy joy returns, for all I know; though it has not happened yet, and it seems unlikely in this moment.

But the Church has been here before, even if I have not. Seeking a faith that will sustain me at this altitude I am beginning to rediscover nourishment in some unfashionable places. I turn again to the so-called liberal theology that formed me as a student, in Birmingham in the 1970s and as a young priest in the 1980s.[59]

At first this surprised me. Those years in Birmingham were a long, long time ago. That was the era of *The Myth of God Incarnate* and *The Remaking of Christian Doctrine* and *The Sea of Faith*, of theologians who are now usually bypassed, usually treated (if they are treated at all) as though all they said and did and prayed and thought was a wrong turn, fit only to be forgotten or at best critiqued.

The days when a man like Professor Maurice Wiles would be invited to chair the Church of England's Doctrine Commission are long over. The days when colleagues of his such as Dennis Nineham and Geoffrey Lampe were invited to join him on the Commission speak of another world. These men, academics, specialists in the Bible and in the writers of the early Church, were shaped by their study into thinkers who, as Yeats said, lack all conviction. But in their time, for me, they were the best.

And to me, breathing the thin air of grief, reaching blindly for the mystery of love, it was these writers who brought comfort, because there was no rhetoric in what they had to say. Their careful caveats, their exploring and their speculating, and by these means their Gospel proclamation, is nourishing me where louder and more confident and certain voices are far away, in the valley, talking of revival fire or of the glories of the parish or of a recovery of certainty; talking to one another but not to me, not today.

No. The quiet, agonised voice, the voice on the far side of the critical furnace, the voice hedged about with qualifications and caveats and yet proclaiming Christ – this is the voice that I need now, and it is one that I have received. Listening to these critical and careful people I find that, like them, I have grounds to be 'confident in the essential truthfulness and trustworthiness of God'.

Instead of the bugle, then, I have the murmuring voices, sceptical, ironic, undemonstrative. I am thinking of some almost-forgotten people, and of some remembered only to be rejected. Almost forgotten: J. Gordon Davies and John Hick and Frances Young from Birmingham. Almost forgotten: Geoffrey Lampe, Maurice Wiles, Dennis Nineham, Leslie Houlden. Forgotten as a teacher of spirituality: Alan Ecclestone.[60] Remembered, if only remembered as a cautionary tale of a bishop gone astray: John Robinson.

And yet Robinson could write this, and in my grief I hear the Gospel in his words: 'The divinity of Jesus was the deed of God. The uniqueness of Jesus was the absolute uniqueness of what God did in him.'[61] And this: 'To assert that 'God is love' is to believe that in love one comes into touch with the most fundamental reality in the Universe, that Being itself ultimately has this character.'[62] And this: 'What evidence is there for such an estimate of the cosmos (that God loves us first)? What indeed, apart from the grace of our Lord Jesus Christ!'[63]

Any of these writers, with their on-the-other-hands and carefully balanced assertions and often-agonised tone, can be mined for statements of this sort, very simple and hard-won statements, iron rations for me in this season. They are as simple in their way as the serene statements of Brother Roger and the Taizé community. If all you have is the records of Jesus, and mystery, and love; and if you want to be intellectually honest, and to walk with the risen and strange Jesus along the road marked by mystery and love, here are some way-markers for you.

And I remember among these people the theologians I knew personally, their gifts to me of care and of a scrupulous honesty lightly worn. I remember Professor Davies' welcome and wisdom when I went to him as a student who was in the midst of what was then called a nervous breakdown, and I remember the small group of Christian radicals to which he pointed me. I remember travelling in a car with Professor Hick to a meeting of the Birmingham group All Faiths For One Race (AFFOR) of which he was the Chair and I the token young person on their Council – travelling with him and hearing his commitment to the messy realities of holding fast to truth in theology and to value in politics; in other words to the mystery of God as the door swings in and out and the cold wind blows; emptiness under the moon. These people's books helped and help me. But meeting them and others like them I met Christians, not books.

My testimony is simply that remembering all these thinkers and the things they wrote brought comfort to me as Kate's health worsened, and speak to me still after she died. And by this way I came to the empty room and the public path, where for now I remain.

In saying these things I have no general point to make. I am indicating aspects of the Christian tradition which have fed me at this time, bearing the experiences I bear. It may be that others who bear similar experiences will find this useful, either as possible resources to explore, or as 'no entry' signs to areas of Christian reflection which will not be helpful. And in referring to those who enjoy a more full-blooded expression of faith I have no criticism to make, unless those people seek to generalise their own rich experience and to demean or marginalise or expel those who do not share it. At the heart of any expression of faith is the encounter with the invisible God. I write more about this when I examine my own years in the valley.

I offer these thoughts with some diffidence. In a conversation last year with a colleague and friend, I was offered a cautionary word, reminded of the occasionally embarrassing books written in later life by ministers whose reading had stopped with their ordination and who felt the need to bring that reading, unreconstructed, to the present day. That is not my intention here. In my generation it was these people. You, reading this, may be of a different generation, and you may have your own people. If not, here are mine as my gift to you. It is the voice (calm, astringent, balanced, faithful) and not the particular speakers that matters most.

In any event you may have a different testimony if you have climbed to the death zone yourself. Or it may be very different for you if and when the moment comes, for you and those close to you. The splintered revelation of God's love is infinitely diverse.

But, just in case, if you find yourself in that high place without any resource, I put the possibility to you that this vein of the church's teaching, this thin, ascetic, questioning tradition, this neglected underground stream, may indeed bring the water of life to a thirsty land. It has been so for me.

All real living is meeting

Feelings go with love, but they do not build love.
Feelings one 'has'; love occurs.
Feelings dwell in man, but man dwells in his love.
This is no metaphor but actuality.
Love is between I and You.
Love is responsibility of an I for a You.
I need a You to become; becoming I, I say You.
All real living is meeting.
(Martin Buber)

Kate and I married in March 1976. She was 19 (20 the next day); I was 22. She was studying for a degree in Drama and Theatre Arts at Birmingham University; I had just graduated with that same degree and was preparing to begin ordination training at the Queen's College, Birmingham. We were married in the Roman Catholic Chaplaincy of Birmingham University, because Kate was Catholic by upbringing; the sermon was preached by the Anglican chaplain.

As part of that marriage service, friends of ours read the lines at the head of this chapter, drawn from various philosophical writings of the Jewish thinker Martin Buber, translated into the English of the West in the last century.

I asked for these lines to be included in our wedding service because of what Martin Buber meant to me. It's not a long story, but it does need a little background. Those who were not arts students in the early seventies may enjoy this glimpse into a forgotten and unrecoverable world ...

In 1972 I had gone to University, the first of my family ever to do so, to study Drama and Theatre Arts in Birmingham. It was a liberation and an adventure to leave home and to experience another and larger city. It was a greater adventure to study drama in an age when the prospectus could say, 'This course involves the investigation of what is at the heart of us, and it can be dangerous'.

Dangerous! As a late-adolescent explorer I wanted little else. I wanted to investigate what was at the heart of me, and never mind the dangers. And so with about fifteen others, mostly older teenagers with a sprinkling of grown-ups in their mid or even late twenties, I threw myself into a series of exercises and explorations, to equip us for inner exploration through physical and emotional theatre.

I remember with my year-group sitting together in pitch darkness and then going outside, wide-eyed in the light, to touch and hug the trees in the University courtyard. I remember looking up with spaced-out eyes and seeing groups of curious students, perhaps of French or Civil Engineering, perhaps even of Theology, looking down with perplexity on us, no doubt asking themselves the perfectly understandable question, 'They're getting a degree for this?'

In fairness I remember more technically rigorous exercises for the voice and the body, and lectures on great playwrights and great theatre practitioners. I remember the sense of security which was the birthright of the students of the early seventies, fully grant-subsidised, utterly sure that somewhere down the line would be a job, and that meanwhile we could explore not only bodies and emotions but also the range of (mostly utopian) political choices that flowed from the late-1960s, living a watery English suburban echo of the flower-children of Haight-Ashbury and of the Woodstock generation.

As Eliot says of a different experience, 'All this was a long time ago, I remember, and I would do it again'.[64] Looking back on all of it now, it is not difficult to mock or to grin or at least to shake the head in pitying bewilderment. But at the time the explorations of the self were real, the sense of growing spiritually as well as emotionally and physically was also real, and strong. In these colder, more pragmatic, more materialistic times I miss that sense, despite all its naïveté, despite all its foolishness.

The doors of the spirit are still there now, as they are in any generation; but the hinges have rusted shut, and ivy has covered them. A willed disenchantment has hardened into the carapace of a grey materialism. But, through the ivy, the doors are there still, less obtrusive, more contended, needing more of a push if they are to be opened, if the surprise is to be received.

All the same it really doesn't do to go hunting for religious treats for their own sake. The party-poppers of the supernatural can blow up in your face. The writers of the Birmingham drama prospectus wrote more truly than they knew when they described the three years of the course as dangerous.

In my second year, open as I was to thinking of the occult, I went to see a film which was gaining some notoriety after its release in 1973 – *The Exorcist* directed by William Friedkin. My mistake was to see it alone, in a half-empty matinée showing; and in this way I met the devil in Birmingham. In the film good triumphs over evil, but at some cost, and only after the devil has had all the best special effects. I left the cinema distressed, and the distress grew into a full-blown anxiety neurosis in the following weeks. I was afraid. It was not that I was afraid of being possessed by evil, though the movie portrayed that with a real and cynical artistry. It was more that my safe and bounded world was suddenly placed in a perspective of radical uncertainty – of what Kierkegaard calls dread. It was the sort of dread that in the end fed on itself and needed no cause or reason, the sort of dread that, in the end, needed medication to be borne.

This neurosis coincided with, and was doubtless fed by, the news that my mother had contracted breast cancer – the first serious (and eventually terminal) illness to have touched my life. Sleeplessness and a constant shapeless fear marked the following months. The medication I was prescribed helped a little, but the damage that had been done was to my sense of ease and entitlement in the world, and like Humpty Dumpty I found that this damage was unmendable. It was out of that distress that a more profound, because far more desperate, spiritual searching was born.

I floundered round the bookshops of Birmingham like a drowning man looking for a lifeline of any kind. And it came in an odd form; a book by (of all people) Malcolm Muggeridge, entitled *Jesus Rediscovered* – the only book on Christianity in the joss-stick-heavy alternative bookshop near my flat.

That a book by the apostle of the so-called Festival of Light should have given me my lifeline is an irony that takes its place among so many in the lives of those who are seeking God. Muggeridge had turned his back on his own somewhat dissolute youth, and had become a self-appointed moralist and spiritual guide, vying with Mary Whitehouse and Lord Longford for the title of least attractive role model for the young. In short he was not at all the guru a young, self-conscious leftie would have chosen – but he was the only guide to hand, and he did indeed guide, though perhaps I did not end up travelling in the direction he himself would have wished.

In any event, his book came as a flickering light through the tangled woods; a light with a promise that previous ways through these woods might after all have their uses. A spiritual path didn't have to be exotic. Perhaps the religion of my childhood was not entirely useless to me in my pain.

As I remember all this now, I bring into focus also a memory from the beginning of my life at University; the memory of being evangelised.

Decades later, evangelism became my specialist subject in the counsels of the national Church. But at the time I received it, it had no meaning for me at all. In my Hall of Residence I was disturbed by a knock on the door and by the appearance of two of my fellow students 'conducting a religious survey'. I invited them in, since at that time I was a paperback Taoist and was happy to share that with anyone who asked. Of course it quickly transpired that the 'survey' was a ruse and that the real purpose of our conversation was for the two guys to tell me about my need for the love of Jesus.

At the time I recognised no such need, though I did know that they were outstaying their welcome. So, when they came to the crisis-point of their pitch and invited me to pray the 'sinner's prayer', I was very glad to do so as a way of getting rid of them. Having repeated the words given to me, admitting my sinfulness and inviting the Lord Jesus into my heart, I rather offhandedly asked the two guys what happened next. They stood up and said, 'We don't know. But we're leaving now; God will do the rest.' And out they went.

And so they evangelised me by leaving. Nothing became their evangelism like the ending of it. I was mildly thunderstruck – not by the fact that they had left, which I greatly welcomed. What counted for me was the evident belief of these young men that God had been listening to our transaction, and that God could be trusted to complete the work that they thought had been begun by the praying of the prayer. They left, and left it to God, and left me bewildered.

I think that this was the first time I had ever encountered any evidence that people could depend on the living God. I cannot remember a single word of the pitch that my evangelists made, nor can I remember the words of the prayer I prayed. But the departure of these people, their belief that God was real and would get to work – this lodged in the mind, and in reading Muggeridge's book the memory returned and the possibility of trust in the invisible returned with it. This was enough to open my eyes. From being a desperate and undifferentiated seeker for meaning and comfort, I became a seeker after truth, and after truth in Christ.

With all these things swirling around I began a course in the Drama Department. It set a course indeed, holding my life and my theological horizons for the next fifty years and more, to this day. In it I encountered a way of thinking and being that transformed my understanding, and from being a seeker after truth in Christ I became a follower. With divine irony this conversion happened through being introduced, by an atheist Marxist academic, to the mind of an agnostic Jewish philosopher, mediated through the discipleship and witness of two professors of Christian theology.

There are those in the Church who grumble about the divorce between academic theology and confessional faith, and who see University theology as an insipid and even a dangerously diluted thing. In my own experience there has never been any such divorce; on the contrary the clear and simple witness of theological thinkers drew me to the Christ who inspired them. My conversion was framed and confirmed by two academic theologians.

It happened like this. In the Drama department we were blessed with a maverick lecturer – one of the only two University lecturers in England, I was told, who had no degree at all. His name was Clive Barker. Clive was an atheist and a Marxist, and a serious man. In his teaching he concerned himself with the big issues – with human mortality, with the Holocaust, with the transformation of the world into a better future (for him it was a future grounded in dialectical materialism).

In the University's Senior Common Room, Clive had fallen into conversation with the head of the neighbouring Department of Theology, the Anglican priest J. G. Davies. And out of that conversation grew a brief one-term course entitled 'Ritual and Drama', a course which brought Professor Davies and his colleague Walter Hollenweger, Professor of Mission in the University and a world authority on the history of Pentecostalism, into the Drama department for an interdisciplinary exploration of the historical roots of drama and the lived experience of encounter.

'Ritual and Drama' was, and remains, the most significant single piece of study in my life. To describe it as 'study' is accurate, but only in the context of the touchy-feely, 'dangerous', emotionally effusive, physically-based ethos of the Drama Department in the early 1970s. We engaged in exercises, in half-night encounter sessions, in shared meals, as well as in lectures on the place of religious ritual in the birth of Western drama and on the philosophy of Martin Buber.

For me, seeking as I was a key to the meaning of my life and of my breakdown, it was a formative time, made all the richer by my falling in love, as students do.

In these colder and harder days, when students before beginning their courses must assess the opportunity cost of a five-figure loan and must weigh against it the benefits of an enhanced salary – in these days the ethos of this sort of shared and fully grant-subsidised exploration seems almost infinitely remote. Yet for me it fulfilled the promise of 'a liberal education' – an education in other words designed to do nothing more useful than to draw out the human being as a being, to develop that being as human.

The Ritual and Drama course was of a piece with the tree-hugging, 'dangerous' ethos of the Drama Department, and I have no doubt that any attempt to replicate it today would fall foul of all University policies, let alone the utilitarian questions of the benefit of the course to future careers. But it shaped my life, and most crucially it gave me a philosophical compass for my explorations of the things of the spirit.

At this time Gordon Davies was just completing a big book, *Every Day God*.[65] His book was written to question and to oppose the very ideas that my embryonic religious experiences might have led me to embrace – in particular the idea that God will primarily, perhaps exclusively, be experienced through the 'numinous' – God as the tremendous and fascinating mystery, the Presence that makes your heart pound, your knees knock, that makes the hairs on the back of your neck rise.

This numinous presence is the Presence of the Piper that terrified and captivated Mole and Ratty in *The Wind in the Willows*:

> Perhaps [Mole] would never have dared to raise his eyes, but that, though the piping was now hushed, the call and the summons seemed still dominant and imperious. He might not

refuse, were Death himself waiting to strike him instantly, once he had looked with mortal eye on things rightly kept hidden. Trembling he obeyed, and raised his humble head; and then, in that utter clearness of the imminent dawn, while Nature, flushed with fulness of incredible colour, seemed to hold her breath for the event, he looked in the very eyes of the Friend and Helper ... and still, as he looked, he lived; and still, as he lived, he wondered.

'Rat!' he found breath to whisper, shaking. 'Are you afraid?'

'Afraid?' murmured the Rat, his eyes shining with unutterable love. 'Afraid! Of Him? O, never, never! And yet— and yet— O, Mole, I am afraid!'

Then the two animals, crouching to the earth, bowed their heads and did worship.[66]

Against this emphasis on the numinous, which is definitively expressed in Rudolf Otto's book *The Idea of the Holy*, Gordon Davies wanted to locate the holiness of God in the everyday – in politics, in art, in sex, most clearly of all in interpersonal relationship. For Davies the numinous was suspect precisely because it was unusual, and because it placed the 'sacred' in a special realm of experience beyond the reach of the 'profane'. It seemed to him (as it seems now to me) that the doctrine of the incarnation, the everyday coming of the Every Day God, tore the veil between sacred and profane and opened the whole of life to the holy. The door swings, God is at once more immanent and more transcendent than is generally supposed.

To a young man struggling with a neurosis based on the fear of supernatural oppression, with a faith reliant on one or two transient religious experiences for a sense of God's goodness, such a wholeheartedly secular, incarnational teaching was both sobering and deeply helpful. In words that came to mean a lot to me: 'I possess nothing but the everyday out of which I am never taken'.

These words are Martin Buber's. He sets them in their context in this passage from his collection of essays, translated into English and published in 1970 with the 1970 title *Between Man and Man*:

What happened was no more than that one forenoon, after a morning of 'religious' enthusiasm, I had a visit from an unknown young man, without being there in spirit. I certainly did not fail to let the meeting be friendly, I did not treat him any more remissly than all his contemporaries who were in the habit of seeking me out about this time of day as an oracle that is ready to listen to reason. I conversed attentively and openly with him – only I omitted to guess the questions which he did not put. Later, not long after, I learned from one of his friends – he himself was no longer alive – the essential content of these questions; I learned that he had come to me not casually, but borne by destiny, not for a chat but for a decision. He had come to me, he had come in this hour. What do we expect when we are in despair and yet go to a man? Surely a presence by means of which we are told that nevertheless there is meaning.

Since then I have given up the 'religious' which is nothing but the exception, extraction, exaltation, ecstasy; or it has given me up. I possess nothing but the everyday out of which I am never taken.[67]

Buber is writing of an episode in his life, in which he spoke with a man in crisis and did not notice the crisis because of his own 'spiritual' state. The young man later took his own life, and Buber never forgot the pain of missing the truth before his eyes.[68]

It is because I read this story as a student that I was pierced by John Drury's acknowledgement a few years later. A Portuguese proverb tells us that God writes straight with crooked lines, and these disconnected and wonky insights have underlined my own search for God my life long. The door swings on to the empty room and onto the path directly into the world as it is – the true God and the real world, unencumbered by a self-consciously 'spiritual' in-between.

Of course there are other ways of viewing the truths of the faith, and indeed the majority of ways pay more attention to this in-between than I have been led to do. But there is also this way; that the overarching theme of Christian theology is incarnational and speaks of redemption as the work of God in the actual, the work of God expressed in the fully incarnate Christ. And to a young man who knew nothing of this language at the time, but who was trying hard to stay sane, Gordon Davies and Walter Hollenweger pointed to a spacious and light path which could be accessed by any human being who was prepared to meet others, and to meet God.

At the time, if these ideas had come to me in conventional Christian language, I would probably have rejected them unexamined. They had an inroad to me because of the drama course and because in *Every Day God* and in his teaching Gordon Davies pointed to Martin Buber's philosophy, and in particular his immensely influential short book *I and Thou*.[69]

Today *I and Thou*, and Buber's work more generally, is relatively obscure. This is a pity. In the late 1960s and 1970s Buber was taken up by many outside the Jewish and the theological/philosophical worlds, because his emphasis on authentic human encounter, on treating other people as 'You' rather than 'It', provided a solid philosophical foundation for the optimistic social vision of the time.

Buber sat loose to the practices of Judaism, while never repudiating them. He spoke instead, in the highly romantic and Germanic idiom of his upbringing, of the need to value the human being infinitely, and to treasure the reality of interpersonal encounter as the royal road to full humanity and to fulfilment of life.

And Buber was the common ground in the conversation in Birmingham between the Anglican Professor of Theology and the agnostic Marxist lecturer in Drama and Theatre Arts.

As my breakdown unfolded, Gordon Davies in particular became for me a pointer to sanity and indeed to community. I went to visit him, in the maelstrom of my anxiety, to ask for help. Unlike Buber, he listened to the crisis and offered a way. He pointed me to a small group of radical Christians, led by one of his colleagues in the Department of Theology; and so for the first time in my life I became one of a group of people who met so that their discipleship might be shared and deepened, their Christian commitment shaped and focused.

Soon after, in my ministry, I became involved with most of the panoply of progressive causes; with the peace movement, following Kate into (what was then called) the Ecology Party, with the recognition of love and holiness in the life of the LGBT+ community, with the anti-Apartheid movement, and so on. I trace the roots of these involvements to that drama course, and those afternoons learning theology from people who wanted to be involved in humankind, and the Jewish thinker who inspired them. Know where you stand, and stand there, alongside those who stand there too whatever their inspiration.

I write this because I want to bear witness to this era, and to this way of being Christian. It is a way which remains valid, though it seems increasingly to be marginal to the life of the churches. And yet for those who walk in it all real living is meeting indeed, embodied and human meeting on the path, nourished by an emptiness which traces the shape of another meeting in the inner space.

In the valley

*We don't seek God's power, we seek His presence.
His power and everything else we need is always
found in His presence.*
(John Wimber)

The air is thick in the valley, and the breathing is easy. On my faith journey I've been here a number of times, though this moment, as I write this, is not one of them.

In the valley you use the language of faith freely and fluently, and you commit to the agreed teachings behind the language wholeheartedly. This is not to say that you 'believe more'. When I think of my years in the valley I don't grieve for old certainties lost. Here I am now in the death zone, but I do not see the valley as a preferred place, still less as a place to be reached by force. The old story I used to tell, teaching about grace in the parish, that 'feelings follow faith', with its illustrations of three eponymous cats on a wall or of a vintage steam railway engine (faith), coal tender (scripture/tradition) and carriage (feelings), was designed to cure people from putting their religious trust in emotion first. Well, it is true; but it could be a deceptive story too. Faith is a gift, and the altitude of faith is a gift too, or at least a function of what happens to you in your life. I do not think that believing is a pure matter of the naked will. Still, the heart of the matter is the encounter with the invisible God, which cannot be fudged by warm feelings.

Kate and I lived in the valley in our years as charismatic Christians, and I lived there for some years before that, when I enjoyed what some are pleased to call 'full-fat Catholicism', loving and exaggerating the cultural 'weirdness' of the faith once delivered to the saints (or at least, delivered to some Anglican saints in the late Victorian era). At other times, long before this present day, I had climbed to a higher altitude, holding the reins of faith more loosely. This was so in my curacy and again for a couple of years in my time in University Chaplaincy and in the first year or two of my time as a parish priest.

But as that time drew to a close, I connected with a friend who was deeply involved in the Vineyard movement, which at that time was beginning to gather strength in the UK. The Vineyard was transitioning from a provider of training conferences to the whole Church into a church-planting movement. Through my friend I came to experience something of the 'paradigm shift' of which the Vineyard teachers spoke,[70] seeing the miraculous, and in particular healing and deliverance, as once more a present reality. These early years of the Vineyard in the UK were not marked by the carnival atmosphere of the Toronto Blessing and its successor waves of enthusiasm. Instead, the laid-back Californian style of John Wimber and his teams chimed effectively with English reserve. Bridge-people such as David Watson and David Pytches further enabled the transition from Los Angeles to the UK.

I am writing about this in order to illustrate what I mean by 'altitude'. Let me say again that I am not describing my experience of these years in order to show how I have outgrown it. Still less do I want to show that everyone must go my way. I know all too many examples of an emotionally reserved Christianity, perfectly good in itself, but cheapened and marred by an ignorant contempt for warm and effusive expressions of faith. Too often this is coupled with an exalting of the modern worldview which gives to some liberal Christians the ability to laugh at phenomena which, for those who experience them, can be liberating and profoundly transformative for the better. I am exasperated by this disdainful rejection of charismatic worldviews and practices. It marks some of the discourse of the liberal church, usually held hand in hand with a high-cultural criticism of 'happy-clappy' music, and tropes of this kind.

As for me, I am glad for my time in the valley, whether adoring the Blessed Sacrament alone in a convent, or singing in tongues with thousands of others in a conference – and of course there are contexts where, with a few score or a few hundred others, it is possible to do both at the same event. The fact that I do not live in the valley any more has nothing to do with 'graduation', as though a higher altitude should imply maturity, or a higher capacity for holiness.

In short I think the whole package of the faith can be taken at any altitude, however much the interpretation of the leap of faith may vary as the air thins or thickens. It is not a matter of cutting away indigestible or lean or fatty parts of the meal. Rather it's a matter of perceiving what Maurice Wiles calls 'Faith and the Mystery of God'[71] with the appropriate language for the appropriate view.

There is a further point to be made about life in the valley. It is not that you 'believe more' there, as if the thickening of the air of faith involves an accretion of doctrines and credulities. In the end, at the heart of any genuine expression of faith, the leap of faith remains. This is so even in the valley, when religious experience is rich and inescapable, like breathing the air in a sauna. At the centre of all that effusion you come in the end to faith, and the mystery of God. The heart of the matter is indeed the encounter with the invisible God, who, like the risen Jesus, will not permit God's self to be touched.[72]

Still, you can't deny that for a pretty zipped-up Anglican in the 1980s the Vineyard's teaching carried a substantial culture shock; the shock of the new. What John Wimber referred to as the 'clinic' – the time in the Vineyard healing conferences after each teaching session, when the Holy Spirit was invoked and the various charismatic phenomena usually manifested – took a little getting used to. In particular the manifestation of 'demonised'[73] behaviour was new to me. But in the light of the 'paradigm shift' in the Vineyard's teaching I was not ready to reject these things out of hand as examples of individual or mass delusion, nor as manifestations of displaced mental illness per se.

Moreover I was deeply impressed by the story told to me by my friend, who attended a Vineyard workshop on deliverance ministry and witnessed there a person whose physical reaction to what was happening inside them issued in projectile vomiting, not a thing normally seen in Methodist Central Hall (though from some reports of his open-air meetings, John Wesley himself may not have been surprised by it). What was impressive about the story was not the vomiting – indeed, my friend reacted to that, as most people would, by standing up and making to leave the workshop. But at the door, glancing back, he saw a young volunteer from the American team peel off his t-shirt and use it to clean up the mess made. This example of pastoral care, from a young person who at their own expense had crossed the Atlantic to help people – this was what impressed my friend as he told me the story. It impressed me in turn.

And in my years as a member and leader of groups sponsored

by SOMA (Sharing Of Ministries Abroad), in Burundi, in Kenya, in Nigeria, I witnessed frequent examples of 'demonised' people who after prayers could be seen 'clothed and in their right mind',[74] with an evident sense of release and of progression in Christian discipleship. the fruit of charismatic prayer. Experiences of this kind can build a readiness to hold together different worldviews, given that what is witnessed can be an evident positive outcome in mental health and adjustment.

This is one aspect of life in the valley, where as Eliot suggested 'prayer has been valid'. Yes, there are many examples of dysfunction and deception in phenomena of this kind. But I have little interest in attempting a general explanation of the medical and spiritual roots of this sort of behaviour. People are complicated, and in this area of life, as in every area, it doesn't help to bring a theological cookie-cutter so that one's own view of human complexity can be stamped on everyone else.

In my theological training, in an overwhelmingly liberal and sceptical environment, the sessions on supernatural evil were taught by the Principal, Anthony Bird, who after ordination had retrained as a medical doctor and who practiced in inner-city Birmingham alongside his work in the college, pioneering a holistic approach to medicine. He began (and in a sense also ended) with the opening words from Psalm 93, 'The Lord reigns!', and his teaching praised the sovereignty of God and also held a respectful distance from overarching psychologies. This befitted a man whose theology was tempered by his weekly work as a GP in multicultural, inner-urban Birmingham, and his contact there with people who explained what was happening to them in many different ways.

In an age when Pentecostal expressions of faith are growing worldwide, and when they increasingly go hand-in-hand with conservative and authoritarian politics, I remember my own very different formation with gratitude. In the previous chapter I describe my first connection with Walter Hollenweger, Professor of Mission in the University of Birmingham, and at the time the world authority on Pentecostal history. Hollenweger had himself been a Pentecostal pastor for many years, before he moved to the Swiss Reformed Church. He had worked with the World Council of Churches as its evangelism adviser, at a time when that organisation was profoundly and controversially radical in its ethos and in its practice. His research led him to speak of a wide range of Pentecostal expressions of church, and he particularly highlighted those allied with liberation movements in the global South. His excellent little book *Pentecost between Black and White*[75] gives a flavour of his teaching. When I absorbed this teaching I was not myself in the charismatic family, but when a few years later I received the baptism in the Spirit and began to minister in that tradition, Hollenweger's subtle and spacious theology of the Holy Spirit was there and waiting for me.

Fundamentally what drew me to the charismatic family was the sense of religious seriousness I found there, wholly irrespective of its cultural expression. I joined a group of charismatic clergy in my town, led by a pastor from the Elim Churches. Members included the pastors of various local new churches, together with a number of Anglican charismatics and others. In its readiness to take God seriously, this group reminded me immediately of the Anglican contemplative order of nuns, the Sisters of the Love of God, with whom I had been involved as a priest-associate since the year of my priestly ordination.

In terms of what I am calling altitude, the Pentecostal group and the SLG Sisters could not have been more different, ranging from the thick, God-spoke-to-me air of the valley in the clergy group to the thinner atmosphere of the high mountain as the plainsong echoed round the convent chapel. Culturally too, the two groups could not have been more different, from the pogo-ing extraversion of the charismatic fraternal (they were of course all men) to the stillness of night prayer in the contemplative community (they were of course all women). But both groups were aligned in their belief in the genuine power of prayer and in the necessity of wholehearted oblation. And both groups were ready to stand on the edge of the present and to trust God for the next second. I felt at home in both; and although the air I breathe is thin now, I still do.

God is more immanent and more transcendent than is generally supposed. If you believe that then you are resigning yourself to waiting on the God who will come to you from the surprising future, in mystery and in incomprehensibility and in love, if the mystical tradition is to be trusted.

In a poem in his collection *Crow*, Ted Hughes coined a phrase which ever since I read it as a student expresses most clearly, for me, how it feels to live immersed in history. He speaks of the world being dark just one inch ahead, of no one knowing what's on the other side, no one knowing what will come in the next unknowable second.[76]

The world is dark one inch ahead. The future is not to be predicted, the future from which the true God comes to us. Speaking of healing prayer, Wimber would say: 'We're called to pray for the sick. Whether or not they are healed is up to God. It's not our job to get God off the hook.' If you have stood or sat with a sick person and prayed expectantly for their healing, you will know that world-is-dark-one-inch-ahead feeling as the silence begins. No wonder so many of us Christians avoid that moment, assuring the sick that we will pray for them in our next 'quiet time' or next church service, when the subject of the prayer is conveniently absent or at a distance. The same vertiginous feeling comes as you enter the silence of imageless meditation. It is no wonder that such moments of intercessory or contemplative silence take courage to face, if we treat them not as a rest from living, but as an encounter with the living God in the purity of faith.

I look back on my time in the valley with gratitude and with affection. I do not regret that I have moved away from it, but nor do wish I were back there. I do not know whether the altitude of my life will change again, but if it does I shall not repine.

None of this denies the fact of toxic theology, wherever it raises its baleful head. A certain flavour of transactional Evangelicalism, balancing the books of the cosmos by means of the suffering of the Son of God, certainly issues in attitudes among some of its leaders which tend towards the bullying and the abusive, and creates atmospheres within which really sadistic abuse can find space to hide. Conversion therapy, and the universe of theological ideas that surrounds it, is a dark perversion of human possibility, fit to be opposed without reservation.[77] The same applies to a romantic Catholicism which looks for saints to follow, and too readily places on pedestals people whose behaviour makes clear that they have no right to live there. The desire of keen people to live 'godly' or 'saintly' lives (depending on their tradition) can be easily twisted.

On the other hand you can be so progressively open-minded that your brains fall out, and all religious seriousness is lost. One of the attractions for me of Don Cupitt's thinking is precisely that all his life he was serious about religion. I have learned a great deal from Cupitt, and shall pay tribute to him in a later chapter, because of his seriousness most of all; but he sometimes seems unusual in the company of less thoughtful and more self-satisfied liberal people who lost the baby long ago, as they tried to help swoosh the bathwater along with the aid of the Zeitgeist.

And of course there are those in the valley communities whose pleasure it is to insult or attack fellow-Christians who breathe thinner air; to attack them for being who they are, just as I have described so-called liberal believers who love to throw bricks in the opposite direction. I do not think that any of this slapstick has anything at all to do with God. It is a distasteful game, and the non-believing cultures of the West love to watch it and thereby to confirm their view that the Christian God is a joke, or at least that many Christian people are.

For all Christian people of religious seriousness, the door opens, into the inner room and onto the public path, and the task remains as it has always been; at whatever altitude, whether travelling within or outwith, to walk by faith and not by sight.[78]

Speaking

Plain speech

*'The weight of this sad time we must obey,
Speak what we feel, not what we ought to say.'*
(William Shakespeare, *King Lear*, V.iii. 323-324)

*'Empires prefer reasoned voices who see it all, who
understand both sides, and who regard polemics as
unworthy of God and divisive of the public good.'*
(Walter Brueggemann, *The Prophetic Imagination*)

*'To speak the truth, and not to mislead others
by our silence.'*
(Episcopal Church, Catechism)

In the late 1980s I was serving as a priest in the High Wycombe Team Ministry, as Team Vicar and later as Team Rector. At that time I was also a national co-chair of the Christian Campaign for Nuclear Disarmament (CCND).

High Wycombe was home to the Daws Hill United States Air Force base, at the time one of the nerve-centres of nuclear planning and response in the event of a war in Europe. A number of RAF bases were located nearby.

On Remembrance Sunday one year I was on the rota to preach. The church, All Saints, 'the Cathedral of South Buckinghamshire', was full, with hundreds of people in uniform, from Beavers and Cubs through to young men in British and American military uniform, accompanied by their senior officers, some of whom bore the responsibility for nuclear response in the event of war. And I was on the rota to preach; I, who believed in the reign of the Prince of Peace and in the absolute moral repugnance of weapons of mass destruction and of the threats that those who have these weapons can make on others in the world.

So I preached; I have no recollection of what I said. Afterwards there was the usual gathering at the war memorial and the remembering of those who died in the wars. And after that, the melée of people greeting one another and catching up with one another, the sort of thing that happens in any regular but infrequent gathering in a fair-sized local community.

It was at this point that one of the political leaders of the town came up to me, to congratulate me on my sermon. 'Well, Paul', he said, 'it wasn't easy, but you've managed to get away without offending anyone today.'

Returning home for lunch, I shared with Kate what this person had said. And I wondered aloud, gloomily; did that ever happen to our Lord Jesus? That at the end of one of his discourses he had been told, 'Well, Jesus, it wasn't easy, but you've managed to get away without offending anyone today'? To put it mildly, it seems unlikely.

It seems unlikely because Jesus had a reputation for plain speech. St John tells us that 'His disciples remembered that it was written, "Zeal for your house will consume me".'[79] They remembered it immediately after Jesus had overturned the tables of the money changers and had told them: 'Stop making my Father's house a marketplace!' They remembered it, in other words, in the context of Jesus' habitual practice of saying what he felt.

Shakespeare's words with which this chapter began, 'The weight of this sad time we must obey, Speak what we feel, not what we ought to say' appear within a couple of lines of the end of his greatest tragedy. After so much death and waste they are spoken by Edgar, the 'good' son of the Earl of Gloucester, who has been deceived and manipulated by his brother Edmund and disowned by his father, who has endured storm and bereavement and conflict, and who has come through suffering to a place of hard-earned wisdom. After all that his words may seem a little simplistic, but they point to a way of being marked by courage.

When I was a working bishop I engaged in the course of episcopal formation provided by the Church at that time. Despite pretty wilful misunderstandings on the part of some church politicians and their followers, this training was not designed to instil a set of managerial skills and jargon, still less to impose a groupthink on the bishops so that they would toe the line and forget their subjectivity. On the contrary it was a value- and virtue-based philosophical education, and as a result of it I was moved to embrace a way of living more fully than I had done to that point. At one point in the training we were invited[80] to identify and to embrace some virtue which we saw as lacking in our lives, but which we hoped (and prayed for grace) to inhabit more fully. In my own case, for a lifetime of reasons, I chose to reflect on courage, and to ask God for grace and strength, and to commit my will, to live more fully in that virtue, and if necessary to pay the price of such living. And for me the exercise of courage was most intimately tied up with the use of plain speech, and with the renunciation of its opposite, 'what we ought to say'.

It was with this in mind that I began to speak more clearly than I had done, in particular about the full inclusion in the community of faith of certain groups who have been and still are excluded. These groups include for example members of the inarticulate working class, or those with profound learning disability, or members of Extinction Rebellion, or faith-questioning and faith-doubting Christians. And also those whose sexuality and gender has not historically been blessed by the Church, members as we would now say of the LGBT+ community.

To speak more clearly about these matters as a bishop in the Church demands a measure of courage, and I doubted mine. So it was for this that I asked God at the Bishops' course in Cambridge.

There is little point in generalising from this personal decision to ask God for public courage. Certainly I have no intention of deprecating those who have made other public choices. A recent Archbishop of Canterbury explicitly refused to say publicly what he thought about matters of human sexuality, knowing that whatever he said would be contentious, giving ammunition to one or other of the church's contending parties. This public announcement of reserve was itself a courageous decision. I respect it, though if I had done the same it would have been for me a falling-short on a commitment made. Where I found myself frustrated was with colleagues in leadership in the churches who gave no public sign whatever, neither of their views nor of their reasons for not sharing them. It seems to me that this behaviour falls under the judgement of the Episcopal Church Catechism when it exhorts believers 'To speak the truth, and not to mislead others by our silence.' The often-repeated slogan that a bishop is to be a sign of unity does not, I think, absolve him or her from speaking truthfully.

To be a bishop in the church, to be seen as a mother or a father in God, is to receive a good deal of infantile projection. Mummies and Daddies are supposed to be perfect; bishops on the other hand are not only imperfect, but very much so. This was borne in on me when in 2017 the church stumbled over yet another rock on the road to inclusion. The bishops had made a corporate statement which had attracted the opprobrium of most of the wider church, but in particular of my progressive friends. I wrote about this at the time, drawing on the thinking of Peter Selby, a previous Bishop of Worcester whom I honour as a mentor and friend for forty-five years. Here it is.

On being an elder: a Via Media reflection, February 2017

'The weak bishops.' 'The lying bishops.' 'The bastard bishops.' 'I wouldn't trust them as far as I can spit.' 'The only way they'll give a straight-line response is if you ask them to design a corkscrew.'

A few months ago on this site (https://viamedia.news) I wrote a piece which spoke of the need for people to express their anger if they were angry.[81] I have seen all the phrases above on social media in the past few days, and I am glad of them, though I am not a masochist and I do not enjoy them. I am particularly grateful to the people who have contacted me directly to express their emotion and to make their points about the recent bishops' statement.

For some, the sense of betrayal is particularly acute when applied to people like me, who have spoken of the need for change in the Church. Where was I? What happened to my voice? How could I have been so weak as to stand with this document?

Twenty-five years ago, in 1991, the same year that *Issues in Human Sexuality* was published, my friend and mentor Bishop Peter Selby wrote a book called *BeLonging*. Its subtitle was *Challenge to a Tribal Church*. In this book Peter spoke of the kind of community the Church is called to be, and contrasted it with the Church as it is. It is a prophetic and an angry book. It locates its anger in three areas; race and racism, gender and sexism, and the treatment of LGBT people. Peter in writing about this last subject drew on his experience of the 1987 Synod debate on the motion proposed by Tony Higton.

And then in the book there comes a chapter called 'The Elders of the Tribe'. It speaks about bishops. It reflects that, when the ordination of women was discussed, 'the report of the House of Bishops on the issue shows strong signs of having been diverted into accepting the agenda of those opposed to the change'. Peter went on to ask, 'Do these responses reflect something of the demands and pressures on leadership when tribal responses are rife?'

This is a very good question. It speaks crisply and clearly over the intervening years.

Peter went on to speak of the risks and dangers inherent in the idea that the bishop is called to be a focus of unity in the Church. He said, 'At the heart of that perception lies one of the most profoundly Christian of instincts, that we are called to bring together and not to divide, to seek and not to lose'. But beautiful and profoundly Christian as it is, Peter said, it is only a half-truth.

His point was that collegiality, the act of standing together and speaking as one, can endanger and indeed exclude the possibility of prophetic dissent. I believe that it is this point that lies behind the anger of the angry today. People believe that the bishops, the bastard bishops, have preferred unity to truth: 'We asked for bread and they have given a stone.'

It is not my intention in this post to defend anyone or anything, least of all myself. In clear awareness of Peter Selby's analysis, I nonetheless stand by the bishops' report. I have chosen to act in this matter wholeheartedly as a member of the episcopal College. I have done so in good faith, because I believe that the suggestions in the report, insufficient as they are, are nonetheless necessary; that they will help LGBT people in the church, will make a church less toxic than the one we have now. But all that is, of course, debatable.

My own experience, since I began speaking out for the beginnings of change in the Church, is that I am profoundly suspected by many who disagree with me and that indeed some of them cannot in conscience remain in the same room as me, or work with me. This has not made me change my mind, but it does help me to understand still further what it is to be a bishop, a bastard bishop, in the Church today.

In October 1986, almost thirty years ago, Peter Selby wrote this in a newspaper: 'Bishops do focus the Church, but what they focus is the Church as it is. Being a focus of disunity is not therefore in itself a sign of pastoral failure.'

I believe that this is so; but since I first read this a quarter of a century ago, long before I became a bishop, I have been most profoundly challenged by the response to Peter's words from another Peter, Peter Walker, then Bishop of Ely, who said this: 'It surely is not a sign of failure, but on one condition; that the disunity which is focused in the bishop is held in a Godward reference. We here touch the mystery, but the central and to a degree the public mystery, of a bishop's prayers …'

The recent statement of the House of Bishops is offered to the Synod in the hope of prayer – not as a finished work but as a resource for dialogue, for further conversation in a context of sharing before God. And in a couple of weeks we shall see what the other Houses of the Synod make of it, what 'the clergy' and 'the laity' make of 'the bishops'. And then the road will go on, and no one's voice will be silenced, as I do not believe mine has been silenced, or will be. And we will continue to learn together what it is to listen, and to dissent, and to pray.

And in this season my prayers will include in particular my LGBT sisters and brothers, inside and outside the Church, whose real-life love has been marginal to our conversation as bishops and whose explicit voice so far has been absent there. And I will pray too for all the Church, and all the bishops, the other bastard bishops like me. And I will continue to seek the right way to be a bishop, in this season on this matter when those who disagree with me outnumber me. I will struggle for a church where the love of the loving will be honoured, whomever they love. I will reach for and advocate for and enable the maximum freedom now, and I'll pray and work and hope for still greater freedom later.

But I would ask one thing of my sisters and brothers in the Church. I am one of 'the bishops', and on many matters I know before God how much I am a bastard bishop. But I also have a name; my name is Paul. Every bishop has a name. If across the Church we are to break the spirit of fear and conformity of which Peter Selby spoke, we must say our names to one another, in the room, in English, looking on the ones to whom we speak. In the Diocese of Liverpool I expect this of the people who share their being in Christ with me; that they will call me by my name and speak the truth to me, and will listen to me as I call their names and speak to them. And each one reading this has a bishop or bishops, each one with a name. I encourage you to learn that name and to use it in a conversation shared. It is in this way that the anger of which I wrote some months ago, the anger I welcome even though it is excoriating to me, will be tempered and used by God to change the world.

∽

Speaking plainly is a Gospel thing, for all its rarity. Public clarity is a proper requirement on public leaders who follow the footsteps of the One whose zeal for the things of God led to his destruction.

I found an image for what I mean in the movie-making advice of the actor Jimmy Cagney. Asked about the art of performance, the great Hollywood star summed up his working philosophy in these words: *'Find your mark, look the other fellow in the eye, and tell the truth.'*[82] There is a lot to be said for this way of being.

'Find your mark ...' Cagney is speaking of the bits of tape, stuck to the floor of a film set out of the camera's sight, which tell the actor where to stand if he or she is to be properly lit and placed. In the movies it helps to find your mark, to know where you stand. And not only in the movies.

The great Jesuit peace campaigner Daniel Berrigan, imprisoned many times for nonviolent civil disobedience in the cause of peace, used to say, 'Know where you stand – and stand there'. It was also he who said, dauntingly for those who speak plainly: 'If you want to follow Jesus, you better look good on wood.'

Towards the end of my working life, the Church of England spent much time in search of 'good disagreement'. That search is spoken about less as I write this, and what is now being sought by the corporate church increasingly seems to be its opposite, bad agreement. Bad agreement would aim to paper over cracks and hold shaky buildings together – until the tremors come, as they surely will. Bad agreement seems to ask for separate jurisdictions, separate bishops, separate networks, all paradoxically in the name of unity. If bad agreement is the goal, then hostages will always be held by those who are threatening to leave the room, or who actually leave the room, replacing the search for fudge with articles in newspapers, open letters, leaked statements and the like. If bad agreement is the goal it will always be possible to stand pat and seek further concessions.

Meanwhile good disagreement demands transparency about

what people think and what they want to see done, and asks what room they will make for those who disagree, in the one body.

Threatening to leave a room strains and splinters the public square, but it also gets you noticed. As the US political commentator David Frum said in *The Atlantic* magazine, speaking of the Republican Party: 'In politics, it's very often the people nearest the exits who claim the most attention.' By contrast good disagreement involves remaining in the room, finding your mark and then seeing who else is there.

'*... look the other fellow in the eye...*' Every age has its 'wicked' problems, 'problems that are difficult or impossible to solve because of incomplete, contradictory, and changing requirements that are often difficult to recognize'.[83] If you're facing these, human connection matters. It is harder to objectify or demonise someone if you face them across a table. Miraculous, rabbit-from-the-hat solutions are unlikely (though with God all things are possible), but surprising convergences and unlikely alliances can emerge from conversations in the room. The partnership between Ian Paisley and Martin McGuinness in Northern Ireland stands as an example from the political world of what can happen when people stay in the room and eyeball one another patiently.[84]

Bad agreement emerges when people do not look one another in the eye, when elephants stand unchallenged in the middle of the room, when a jaunty and distant politeness takes the place of an honest conversation.

'*... and tell the truth.*' A frustrated diplomat once said that the people he was meeting 'do not think what they feel, do not say what they think, and do not do what they say.' Bad agreement emerges when people for whatever reason – a quiet life, fear, confusion, ulterior motive – do not tell the truth to themselves or to others.

To tell the truth is to make yourself vulnerable, because you could be wrong. Anyone who faces another in a room of disagreement should be saying to themselves, as well as to the other, the words that Oliver Cromwell spoke to the Scottish Church Assembly: 'I beseech you, in the bowels of Christ, think it possible you may be mistaken. Precept may be upon precept, line may be upon line, and yet the Word of the Lord may be to some a Word of Judgment; that they may fall backward and be broken, and be snared and be taken!'.[85] Or as the Marxist Rosa Luxembourg put it: 'Freedom is always and exclusively freedom for the one who thinks differently.'

At any given moment it helps conversation if you communicate what you believe to be true, even though you're open to a change of mind. And the truth is not always sharp and clear. Communicating an honest confusion is better than communicating a false clarity. It helps then to remain in the room with others, and openly to share the truth you have to share. To do so is to move either towards understanding and agreement, or towards understanding and good disagreement.

Agreement is lovely, if it is indeed agreement; if it is the end of a journey and not a fudged way-marker on the road to a quiet life. Too often however, in the words of my friend Shannon Johnston the retired Bishop of Virginia, 'Agreement is over-rated'. Cheap, hasty, quiet-life agreement is over-rated. It is a piece of paper held in the hand and waved about with words about peace in our time. And in the end it fails, and returns us to the remote and tribal mud-slinging that marks our political and ecclesial discourse in these days. By contrast good disagreement is a disenchanted but human possibility, demanding patience and forbearance, from which divine surprises may indeed emerge, but which does not prescribe them in the name of unity.

Speak plainly; find your mark, look the other person in the eye, and tell the truth. To do so is to contribute to the building of the public square once again. In the splintered, fractious social and political climate in which we are compelled to live today, surely by God's grace this is the least we can do together.

In my working life, I did my best to act in this way and to speak about it to my colleagues – with whatever success, because I did not do it as well as I might have, and in any case success is not guaranteed. And preparing my sermon on the door I found John 16 given in the lectionary, and I said this:

> … the word translated 'plainly', in the language of the Bible is parrhesía. His Holiness Pope Francis has commended this word. He has frequently said that only a church marked by parrhesía, by plain speech, by truthful speech, is a church worth having, and I agree with him. Parrhesía is the Bible's word, it's the Pope's word, it's the very the word on which I spoke at our clergy retreat day last year, and it's the word that the lectionary has given me today.

It points to a way of speaking, and a way of being. You can see people who live that way. In the life of a man like Desmond Tutu, the greatest Anglican bishop of our times, you see one who lived that way.

In the spirit of this word and of those who live it, I invite you to walk this same way. Speak plainly. Fudge is sweet; but it's not a nourishing food.'

The naughty step

*'You sound sceptical'. The guy smiled again. 'Of course
I'm sceptical,' he said. 'I'm an Anglican'.*
(Lee Child, *Nothing to Lose*: Jack Reacher #12)

Unhappy the land that needs heroes.
(Bertolt Brecht, *Galileo*)

Christians are prone to hero-worship, in some ways making Brecht's point. We are drawn to people who have followed Jesus in ways that challenge and encourage us, and they become our heroes. Whether we embrace the public gallery of the Saints and the Calendar, or whether we construct our own private list, building pedestals for heroes is something we're good at.

I suppose every Christian has such a private list of acquaintances, friends or family members whose lives are or were in one way or another radiant with the love of God. These lives are indeed heroic, to be celebrated and hopefully to be emulated, as we all seek to grow in holiness with our eyes on one another's example as well as on the Lord's. But it is not that sort of heroism that I want to address here.

My list of heroes falls into two broad categories, though some of them qualify for both. There are those whose witness has resulted in political and public controversy. And there are those whose reflections on God, whose theology, has led them to a place of notoriety, from which they have faced the active hostility of their fellow Christians. Each of these categories can lead you to the naughty step.

As I write, the Episcopal bishop of Washington DC, Mariann Edgar Budde, has just preached at a National Service in her Cathedral, attended by the newly-re-elected President Donald Trump. In it she made a plea for mercy; a plea which earned her the epithet 'nasty woman' from the President. In a polarised world, some people saw Bishop Mariann's sermon as an abuse of a platform which should have been used for more spiritual or state-sanctioned words. Many others (including myself) saw her sermon as a prophetic and courageous example of speaking truth to power, and paying the price in the coin of contempt and hostility from the powerful and their allies.

Bishop Mariann (who wrote a book a couple of years ago called *How We Learn To Be Brave*[86]) has become a hero of the progressive Church, though for many politically conservative people she is excoriated as a foolish and mistaken woman, fit only to be corrected and/or pilloried, in short placed on the naughty step.

To be a Christian witness and to be on the naughty step are frequently linked, and this should be unsurprising to readers of the Gospels who have heard Jesus say things like, 'you will be dragged before governors and kings because of me, as a testimony to them and the gentiles. When they hand you over, do not worry about how you are to speak or what you are to say, for what you are to say will be given to you at that time, for it is not you who speak, but the Spirit of your Father speaking through you.'[87]

In the last few years I have been re-examining and weighing my list of those who are heroes of faith to me because of what they thought and wrote as well as what they have done. I am trying to make sense of faith in my retirement and in my grief, and as I do so I certainly look to those who speak truth to power, and you will see one or two mentioned in the paragraphs below. But among my heroes I have turned with especial interest to those who are not necessarily notorious beyond the church, but who have simply followed the train of their thoughts or the way of their prayers, attempting to be honest about life and about God as God seems to them. They have found themselves on the church's very own naughty step as a consequence of their theology. And as I remember the few and mild times when I was on the naughty step myself, I thank God for those who preceded me there and whom I respect. They are heroes to me.

It's true that, like everywhere else, the church has its share of people who are simply contrarian, or controversialist. The church has its share too of publicity-seekers and if you seek publicity, the naughty step is one place to find it. And of course people are complicated, Christian theologians not excluded, and people's motives are thoroughly mixed.

So in my personal discernment I have asked myself: what is it that leads me to look to some as heroes of the faith because of their theology? I find that it is not to do with their fluency in language, or clarity and beauty of thought, important as these things are. In the end the assessment for me, the acid test of authenticity in faith, is to be found in the company one keeps. It was so for Jesus. If you're on the naughty step, for whose benefit do you say and do the things that get you opposed?

Here's an example of what I mean. I'm writing these words on the day after Don Cupitt died, and I was privileged to attend his funeral a few weeks later.[88] As a University chaplain in the mid-80s I wrote to him, thanking him for his book *The World to Come*[89] (the follow-up to his famous *Taking Leave of God*, followed by literally scores of others). He kindly replied with a postcard agreeing with my high opinion of the Indian philosopher Nagarjuna and encouraging me to keep on thinking. This was at a time (like most times, actually) when thinking was beginning to be seen as a risky occupation for a priest. Don urged me not to be intimidated by the klaxons of a self-proclaimed orthodoxy. 'There's quite a lot of us really', he wrote.

Earlier I have spoken of the priceless gift to me of the careful, agonised liberal theologians of my youth, with their endless caveats and qualifications, shining through which was their tempered, stripped-down, demonstrably indestructible commitment to the faith, and the life of faith. That faith was reduced in the sense that a sauce is reduced, and was all the tastier for that. But Don Cupitt was cut from another cloth. His was a robust and unapologetic radicalism, of the sort that attracts and sometimes actively seeks opposition. He was well equipped for such a role.

Writing once of C. S. Lewis (for whose theology he had very little time) he ended his critique: 'But at least Lewis wrote well'. Surely anyone can say the same of Don. I am told by those who were personally taught by him that his expositions on their essays were known as 'Donologues'. His books may be seen as extended Donologues, as his fluent, readable prose stretched across his many volumes, a distinctive voice outlining a radical non-realism which sustained him, and from time to time sustained me, and more others than you might think. There's quite a lot of us really.

His thinking developed over the decades, but it never strayed far from the non-realism which made him famous in 1984, when his BBC series *The Sea of Faith* was released. At the time I was a University chaplain in West London, and my ministry mostly comprised a long series of discussion groups each week, at breakfast in Halls of Residence, at lunchtime in University departments, in the evening in community houses of students whom we placed from year to year in London Vicarages while the Diocese was deciding what to do with the properties in the longer term. These discussions took place with students whose minds were sharp and whose readiness to explore was unlimited. In some of these groups, for some months, Cupitt was the subject of discussion. He was not new to me. In 1980, the same year I was ordained priest, I had read his *Taking Leave of God*,[90] a book which had challenged and shaken the more shakeable parts of my inherited religious habits of thought. *The World to Come* followed, and remains one of my favourites among his many books (the other favourite, *Mysticism after Modernity*,[91] is supremely a book linking the desert and the empty room on the one hand, with the secular world in all its light and splendour).

You don't need to agree with everything Don wrote, or indeed with much of it, in order to be helped by him. If you read him with a receptive mind he will tighten your thinking, scraping the barnacles from the ship with which you sail the sea of faith. At least it was so for me.

Theologians on the naughty step are often cancelled, which is a pity. But whether it's Meister Eckhart in the thirteenth/fourteenth centuries, or Don Cupitt in the twentieth/twenty-first, the voices of those who are comfortable with the unknowable need to be heard. Reading Eckhart and Cupitt I am reminded that God is more transcendent and more immanent than is generally supposed, and the fully human and fully divine Jesus will not be threatened out of existence by radical philosophical theology.

Christianity is a mystery religion, though the mystery is not to be found in the odd and (what Kate used to call) 'woo-ey' places that the word can conjure up. Seeking God in a weird, fenced-off, religious midway-place is a fruitless prospect if what you seek is the salvation of the world. The starkness of God's unknowability confronts anyone who has prayed in silence, or prayed for healing or for the peace of the world. God is a mystery, even or perhaps especially for those with a high doctrine of revelation. It must be so if the Bible is to be trusted.

God's voice comes to us in Isaiah:

> For as the heavens are higher than the earth,
> so are my ways higher than your ways
> and my thoughts than your thoughts.
> For as the rain and the snow come down from heaven
> and do not return there until they have watered the earth,
> making it bring forth and sprout,
> giving seed to the sower and bread to the eater,
> so shall my word be that goes out from my mouth;
> it shall not return to me empty,
> but it shall accomplish that which I purpose
> and succeed in the thing for which I sent it.[92]

And more simply and starkly comes the voice of the Johannine community, coming to us twice in scripture: no one has ever seen God. No. One. Has. Ever. Seen. God.

In addition to the truth of this invisible God I have mentioned Ted Hughes' words as a crystallisation of what it is to live in time: 'The world is dark one inch ahead'. To be faced with the divine unknowability, and the perpetually unknowable future, is to stand in need of guides. And for me, a guide into the silence has been Don Cupitt, who affirmed the mystery of God even in the midst of his many denials, perhaps even despite himself. And he faced opposition from other Christians because of what he wrote and said, ranging from book-length, reasoned rebuttals of his thinking to simple dismissive abuse.

With Don in mind I want to honour other Christian theologians who face opposition and who sit on the naughty step, and from time to time I want to sit there with them, because they have been so helpful to me. The history of the Church offers you many examples: Origen, Pelagius, Johannes Eckhart, Jeanne Guyon, George Tyrrell, John Colenso, Ivan Illich, Alan Watts. A small selection of the kind of person I mean from my own lifetime: from England Don Cupitt and David Jenkins, from Scotland Richard Holloway and Elizabeth Templeton and Marcella Althaus-Reid, from New Zealand Lloyd Geering and Alan Jamieson, from the USA Jack Spong and Marcus Borg and Carter Heyward and Robert Funk and John Dominic Crossan.

Many of these people may have been in many ways mistaken. Saying this I recall the Japanese mathematician Goro Shimura, speaking of a deceased friend. Shimura said: 'As a mathematician he made a lot of mistakes. But he made mistakes in a good direction... I tried to imitate him but I found out that it is very difficult to make good mistakes'.[93]

The people on my list did not form a movement, and indeed they didn't agree among themselves about much; but I believe they thought bravely and they wrote well, and if they made mistakes then they were usually mistakes in a good direction. Like Philip Larkin whom I shall discuss in a moment, in the quality of their language they evoked more than their often-reductionist explanations could pin down.

Other figures sat, and sit, on that step too: the monk and wide ecumenist Thomas Merton, whose conversations with radical political activists and Zen Buddhists among others made him an uncomfortable voice for those in the Church who had simply assumed that as a monk he was bound to be a good boy; the joyful and irrepressible bishop Desmond Tutu, the finest and most significant Anglican bishop in the world in my time, who pushed the boundaries of Christian acceptance over and over, welcoming the unloved as summed up in his book *God is Not a Christian*.[94] The quiet and courageous voice of Lawrence Freeman, another monk of the silent place and the courageous voice, whose leadership of the World Community for Christian Meditation gives him the freedom to say radical things quietly and clearly. The peace activist and nonviolent pioneer Daniel Berrigan SJ, whose opposition to the Vietnam war was only the most visible of his many stands taken for the oppressed and against the comfortable. It was he whose phrase 'Know where you stand, and stand there' became almost a mantra for me in my own reaching-after what it is to follow in the steps of the Lord Jesus. Many of these people sat on the edge of the institution, and a few spoke from the centre of church life; all of them polarised opinion.

Do these voices, these people, have anything in common beyond the suspicion with which they are or were so often treated? I think they do. Each of them in their way has opened the door and stepped into the desert room or on to the path that bypasses what John Stott used to call 'Christian rabbit holes' and leads directly to the world as it actually is. To pass through this door is to stand with sometimes-strange allies; and maybe with them, sometimes, to sit on the naughty step.

Richard Holloway, like Desmond Tutu, was an Archbishop in the Anglican world. In his wonderful autobiography *Leaving Alexandria*[95] he unfolds the story of his life, underlining the time spent at Kelham's monastic community and theological college, speaking most movingly of the chapel and its little door through which alumni of Kelham left the community to seek Christ in the world and to live and work alongside Him there. Holloway's journey carried him away from that way of being a Christian, and more recently away from the need to admit that he was a Christian at all; but the lessons of the silent room never left him, and gave him the courage to keep on thinking and to keep on growing as he aged.

David Jenkins was a nuanced, carefully orthodox theologian who could not help himself when it came to making headlines. He said that, '[the Resurrection] is real. That's the point. All I said was "literally physical". I was very careful in the use of language. After all, a conjuring trick with bones proves only that somebody's very clever at a conjuring trick with bones.' These words were shaken, stirred and then served up to indicate the heresy of a bishop who could say that conjuring tricks with bones summed up the central reality of the Faith.

The *Church Times* felt the need, in the light of the many letters it received, to reassure its readers about Jenkins. 'Thanking the paper for its support, Jenkins wrote to say that his apostolic responsibility was not to defend credal formulae, but to explore and expound "the great Catholic symbols in the light of the best current knowledge".'[96] That works for me. But for these and other reasons Jenkins was therefore on the naughty step at the time of his episcopal ordination, and when York Minster was struck by lightning three days after that event, there were those who made much play of God's retributive anger (though less was said about the thunderbolt's rather sloppy timing).

John Shelby Spong, for many years bishop of Newark New Jersey, was an unabashed liberal, who tried in book after book to unfold a version of Christian faith which could be harmonised with modernity. He was inevitably accused of selling the pass on the Christian faith and of watering its doctrines down so as to win acceptance among American liberals like himself. But rereading Spong's work today I'm reminded of the words of Archbishop William Temple to Ronald Knox in 1913: 'I am not a spiritual doctor trying to see how much Jones can swallow and keep down; I am more respectable than that; I am Jones himself asking what there is to eat.'[97]

Jack Spong wanted, himself, to be a Christian without internal compromise and without external contradiction, and he saw it as his mission to help those who had left the faith behind for the (no doubt Boomerish) reason that it was intellectually impossible for them to remain in the Christian family. His rather pugnacious temperament led him to make himself comfortable on the naughty step, and maybe from time to time he said or wrote things which were explicitly designed to fluff up the cushions there. But fundamentally he was Jones, asking what there was to eat, and in his day a great many people testified to the value of the questions he asked. I too honour those questions, and I value his answers (even if the nature or tone of those answers is a bit indigestible from time to time).

In these 'post-liberal' days it may be that there is no room in the Anglican Communion for John Robinson, or for David Jenkins, or for Don Cupitt, or for Jack Spong, or for Richard Holloway, and if so, there is no room for me. I cannot bring myself to worry about that.

One more name, this time from well outside the family of faith. I'm writing about him in the hope that you may draw the parallels, and find for yourself others who have helped you from the margins, and also so that you can rediscover or discover this particular person for yourself; a poet whose poetry is perhaps spiritually wiser than the man himself allowed himself to be.

Some months after Kate's death I made a strange pilgrimage – to Hull and Holderness, places I had never been, purely so that I could walk the Larkin Trail.[98]

Philip Larkin was not a radical theologian, at least not in his own mind. His opinion of religion, after reading the Bible through for a year, a section every morning while shaving, was simple enough: 'It's absolutely bloody amazing to think that anyone ever believed any of that. Really, it's absolute balls. Beautiful, of course. But balls.'[99] More specifically in his late poem 'Aubade', he described religion as a vast moth-eaten musical brocade, created to pretend we never die.[100]

Whenever Larkin caught himself writing transcendently he would try to reclaim his self-constructed persona as a grumpy old provincial atheist, undercutting himself with acerbic and profane commentary, for example in a note on his poem 'The Arundel Tomb':

'Love isn't stronger than death just because statues hold hands for 600 years'[101] or in case that was too subtle, 'In his workbook, the final three words of "High Windows" – "and is endless" – are replaced by "and fucking piss".'[102]

And yet God is everywhere. And the fact is that the poet in Larkin refused to mock in public what he had written for the public. And so he ended his collection 'The Whitsun Weddings' with 'The Arundel Tomb' and the thought of love surviving, which as Andrew Motion says in his biography[103] contained a charged rhetoric with a life of its own that lifted the line out of whatever deprecations Larkin tried to throw at it, so that it is carved today on many headstones, including Larkin's own memorial in Westminster Abbey.

And at the end of the title poem of his final collection, "High Windows", having delivered himself of some curmudgeonly reflections on birth control and sexual liberation, he goes on to surprise us (and himself I think), and to complete the poem by thinking and speaking of light, and of the sun on windows, and he reflects on the emptiness of the blue air, showing nothing, located nowhere, being endless.

Larkin's reflection is not by any means an act of faith. But nor is it 'and fucking piss' after all. From the depths of himself he writes words which transcend any atheist doctrine, words which look to emptiness and brightness, words which have more in common with Meister Eckhart than with Humanists UK.

This man – Larkin – as spiritual guide? Well, yes. If the mystery and the incomprehensibility of God strikes you strongly in any given year, I recommend that you walk the Larkin Trail, round the post-industrial city of Kingston upon Hull and round the Holderness coast of East Yorkshire, and especially that you brave the strange, shifting landscape of Spurn Point (on the days and at the times when the tides permit you to do so). When I visited Spurn it was wintry and murky and snowing and as far as I could see I was the only person there. The North Sea, brown with the silt that forms Spurn Point, looked like churning leather. And I stood there, on the narrow spit of land, looking east into the sea through the blizzard, and west into the empty Humber, and I felt as I think Soren Kierkegaard did, flying as the alone to the Alone, or as Henry Williamson did, 'seeing the tears of Christ breaking on the stones of the world'.[104] Strange heroes, strange guides who can lead you to strange places, yet after all God is everywhere.

This list is mostly pale, male and stale, as I am myself. I am a child of my time, and like Nicodemus I cannot re-enter my mother's womb and be born. In these days, now that the day to day pressures of work are lifted from me, I am trying to expand those horizons. And of course I find that theologians who are women, or queer, or of Global Majority heritage, are placed on the naughty step more quickly, and respected even less. As I age and before I die, I hope to hear from them more, and to recognise courage and clarity wherever it may be found, and to sit with them if I can and if they will have me.

'Unhappy the land that needs heroes.' For a Christian the example of Jesus is, in the end, the only one that matters; and others both within and beyond the Faith are only to be respected if their lives and their words echo his. In the end it was for his theology that he was crucified. And for any Christian there is nothing special about the theological naughty step unless we might find Jesus, too, sitting there. The people I have listed here, and others like them, sat on the naughty step more or less regularly, and some of them camped out there permanently. The prevailing spirit on that step was and is robust, wholehearted, unafraid. And I value the naughty step because I see in these things an affinity of the spirit with Jesus himself, who can be said to have pioneered the naughty step for our community of faith, and to have been the first to die on it.

On ...

On love and anger

I was honoured when part of this reflection (the part in italics on p.114) was turned into a poster by One Body One Faith. The wider piece tries to make proper room for anger in a fully discipled life. If proper room is not made, anger will break out as uncontrolled fury or manipulative passive-aggressive rage, as I'm afraid we have recently seen more and more in the church and in the world.

Like many of the pieces in this section, this one began life as a Via Media reflection (https://viamedia.news). The Via Media blog was created by Jayne Ozanne, whose untiring advocacy and naming of truth, in the area of sexuality and in many other areas, has blessed the Church for many years, and still does to this day. As I write, the blog itself is superbly edited by Helen King.

'That's what politics is about, Philip; love and anger.'
Neil Kinnock to Philip Gould, 1992

'That constant humiliation to survive. If you're not angry about it, what kind of person are you?'
Ken Loach, 2016

'Don't mourn, organise!'
Joe Hill (to a friend before he was executed), 1915

What motivates people to make a difference? What motivates people to return, day after day, in the face of discouragement and misunderstanding and opposition, to make a difference again? And to keep on making a difference until things are different? How do we find the strength inside?

The road to justice and holiness begins from our own front

door. If as a Christian I believe I am beloved of God, and if I believe God made me the way I am, then my jumble of emotions, desires, longings and hopes is God-given and capable of redemption. From there the journey begins, the journey to change the world inside and outside. Kieran, one of the leaders of 'Open Table', our LGBT+ congregation in Liverpool, told me this week of a saying they have there: 'Come as you are. Be as you are. Leave differently.'

All this is true. But the Christian tradition has often been suspicious of anger, excluding it from this vision of the whole of life redeemed, expecting disciples to amputate it or repress it or ignore it, at any rate to suspect it and fear it, to regret it and deplore it and certainly not to listen to its voice and amplify its cry. There is a story of one of the saints of early monasticism, in the desert of northern Egypt, who kept a stone in his mouth for many months 'until he learned to speak without anger'.

For much of the church and much of the time, to be angry has been the same as to be immature. In such a view anger must be bottled up, we must hedge the heart before we speak; the only thing that matters in our conversation is argument, dispassionate argument. In such a view argument is what makes a difference, argument is what moves and changes people, only argument. After argument there can be no room for feeling, only argument moves the world and the church family along, we were born to argue and then to submit to the better argument. Let's keep everything cool and cerebral; after all, didn't Jesus say that the angry would be subject to judgement (Matthew 5:22)? The heart is above all things deceitful (Jeremiah 17:9) – so let's strangle it, in particular shrivel its terrible twin faces of anger and desire.

And yet, and yet. We know that the Bible makes more room for anger (and of course desire) than this. The Lord Jesus does not seem to have been ashamed of his anger, when he cleared the temple or when he healed the man with a withered hand or when he spoke hard and straight truth to the Pharisees (John 2:13ff, Mark 3:1ff, Matthew 23:15ff). The writer of Ephesians was unafraid of anger, and distinguished it clearly from sin (Ephesians 4:26f).

No, anger is not sin – though of course anger is seen in scripture as potentially dangerous and as in need of care. James, echoing a recurrent theme in the Hebrew bible, exhorts his readers to be 'slow to anger' as God is slow to anger (James 1:19, Exodus 34:6, Numbers 14:18, Nehemiah 9:17, Psalm and Proverbs passim). But the scriptures make room for the slow heart, for slow and real anger just as much as for passionate desire.

So what motivates people to make a difference? What motivates people to return, day after day, in the face of discouragement and misunderstanding and opposition, to make a difference again? And to keep on making a difference until things are different? Love and anger.

In his marvellous question-and-answer *Catechism of Christian Doctrine*[105] the Roman Catholic theologian Herbert McCabe writes this:

Q: What is courage?

A: Courage is a disposition of our feelings of aggression which inclines us, characteristically, to face up to and deal with difficulties and dangers for the sake of doing what is good: a courageous person is neither over-aggressive nor timid; is angry about the right things at the right time and is prepared to suffer patiently when it is necessary and even to die for the sake of justice or in witness to the gospel...

Q: How do we exercise the virtue of courage?

A: We exercise the virtue of courage principally in energetic struggle on behalf of the poor and the weak and on every occasion when we have to face hostility and danger for the sake of justice and the gospel.

In short, as McCabe says in his book *On Aquinas*: 'Courage is the virtue by which our aggression is reasonable'.[106] And in every deep and deep-felt conversation in the world and the Church, our aggression needs to be reasonable. Not strangled, but strongly present. And reasonable.

I write this for a purpose – to combat poor practice in the Church. The poor practice is this; that people whose inner and outer lives are deeply impacted by an issue, and who become angry as a result, are discounted precisely because of their anger. This has been the age-old fate of women in the West, and the fate of any oppressed group, and it is the fate of many LGBT+ people in the Church today. The advice from the men at the top (and they usually are men, and they are always at the top) is the old, infuriating, demeaning advice: 'Calm down, dear'.

Calm down, and clam up. Don't feel what you feel, or at least don't express it. Behave. Let's have a 'debate', let's hear an argument, not a cry. Deny your deepest pain, and your deepest love. Instead play our game, our arguments-only game, our game that believes people only really exist from the neck up; calm down, dears, because your game is not legitimate, and we have decided that, and we are always right.

In the face of this old and cold advice I want to offer an even older, warmer, biblical encouragement to those on the edge in the churches, and in this season to LGBT+ Christians in particular: be warmly angry, be hot with anger, but do not boil away.

> *Be warmly angry. Be hot with anger, but do not boil away. Feel what you feel, and turn the feeling into strength. Don't mourn, organise. Let the person you are in God speak out, so that your own desires and your own anger become the engine for a just world.*
>
> *Come as you are. Be as you are. Leave differently. Love differently. Bring your heart's desire to bear on the life of our community. Make yourself heard, and if people like me act as if we know you better than you know yourself, then set us to rights, tell us the truth, motivate and stir and provoke us to know your anger as you know it.*
>
> *And then, please, for all our sakes, exercise your courage, the virtue by which your aggression becomes reasonable. And bring your courage to bear on the councils of the church. And share facts and logic and truth and history and perspective, and (yes, of course!) argument. But never lose your anger, even after you've let it blow through you as the sun goes down, and refused to allow it to consume you. Bring your next-morning anger, your tempered anger, your reasonable passion, the truth of how you feel, and contribute it to the whole community, which desperately needs to listen to it.*
>
> *Make a difference. Return, day after day, in the face of discouragement and misunderstanding and opposition, to make*

a difference again. Keep on making a difference until things are different.

And thank you for bearing with us still, and for enriching our half-awake lives, and for waking us up further. And thank you most of all for the passionate word of Christ that you have received and that you – and only you – can speak forward into our church's symphony today, a word of the heart, the word of love and anger.

On being inclusive

A Christmas reflection for Via Media, written in my last Christmas as a serving bishop, on a much-contended word.

Do not fear what they fear, and do not be intimidated, but in your hearts sanctify Christ as Lord.
(1 Peter 3:14,15a)

It's not that long ago that the word 'inclusive' used to irritate me. I saw it as a party slogan, rather like the use of 'orthodox' or 'godly' in other parts of our Church. It annoyed me, even as it nagged at me.

This is because I hoped to rise above such divisive words. In particular, in my early days as a bishop I tried to inhabit a vacuum of opinion. I believed that this vacuum is the proper place for a bishop, the only place that a 'symbol of unity' in the Church could possibly sit. Such a vacuum is certainly a good place to live if you want a quiet life: in space, no one can hear you scream.

Well, over the years things changed for me. As with so many others in the long history of the Church, events and wounded people approached me and I came to know them, and they changed me. Now, as I approach my retirement, the place and voice of a disciple involves (to quote Dan Berrigan SJ as I so often used to do), 'knowing where you stand, and standing there'.

So I have done my best to say what I think about a whole range of things, including one or two which are contended in today's church. I've tried to speak for, to make room for, the lives of people for whom there was no room in the past. Overall I've tried to set my compass by what the Roman Catholic Church has called the preferential option for the poor; what my predecessor David Sheppard called the bias to the poor.

As I've done so there has been no shortage of people to tell me that by making this journey at all, I have fallen short of my discipleship in general and of my episcopal vocation in particular.

I'm told that I have gone wrong in one or both of two ways: by being a heretic and/or by being a maverick.

Those who think I'm a heretic usually write to me. They tend to be unrestrained in the use of their language. Many of them believe that my eternal destiny is at stake and that they need to help me with my salvation by setting me straight. From the tone of their letters they clearly believe that the job will best be done by shaming me into heaven, reminding me forcibly of my mistakes, inaccuracies, ignorances, underlining how offended they are by my words. I try always to reply to these letters and emails with thanks, but I have to say that none of them has yet succeeded in its aim. Shaming and anger are poor persuaders.

Those who think I'm a maverick are usually more restrained in their style. They tend not to write but to speak privately, or to express themselves non-verbally, in the raising of an eyebrow of the rolling of an eye. They communicate more in sorrow than in anger. What a pity, brother, that from time to time you have so noisily flouted the agreed norms of polite Christian behaviour. How unfortunate that you seem to be questioning or resisting or pre-empting the necessarily slow deliberations of the Church. What a shame that you keep banging on about one or two issues, rather than spreading your indignations more carefully, seamlessly and evenly about the place. How sad that you're so ... well, untactful.

For me, as for a number of my colleagues retired and serving in all orders of the Church, being seen as a maverick is unpleasant and unwelcome. Unwelcome, since our belief is that we live in the mainstream of discipleship and not on its margins. Making the option for the poor, being there for those on the edge of things, is the mainspring of our witness. But we ourselves do not wilfully seek to be on the edge of things. Still less do we want to be treated as a mildly tolerated presence on the edge, like pepper in a stew, piquant but mercifully optional.

Anyway, as the year's end approaches, and with around fifty days to go before my farewell service in Liverpool, I have been reflecting on this question: how have I, who used to be so annoyed by the word 'inclusive', come to be seen by many as an annoying maverick/heretic now?

Perhaps it's because I have entered in to a greater faithfulness to what I was taught about God and about his only-begotten Son. That at any rate is my hope and prayer.

Here is a short passage from the Lutheran liturgical theologian, Gordon Lathrop. I read it years ago, and I quote it often:

> Draw a line that includes us and excludes many others, and Jesus Christ is always on the other side of the line. At least that is so if we are speaking of the biblical, historic Christ who eats with sinners and outsiders, who is made a curse and sin itself for us, who justifies the ungodly, and who is himself the hole in any system.[107]

In the week of my forty-second Christmas as an ordained minister, I look again as a disciple to the paradox of the Incarnation. I look to the Infant of Days, to the scrap of humanity who couldn't find a room yet who is fully God, who grew up to dine with sinners, to scandalise the religious, to die an unclean death outside the city. I look to him and I agree with Gordon Lathrop. Jesus is himself the hole in any human system of righteousness, and Divine righteousness is a gift given to those on both sides of any line. And I will live in this mystery with all the integrity I can muster.

Another long-remembered thing. As a student I read a book by Daniel Berrigan SJ, the US Catholic priest and peace protestor whose words I quoted above. The book was called *America is Hard to Find*.[108] That book drew me into the peace movement, as a member of which I was honoured to have been arrested and held three or four times for standing or sitting in the wrong place, with Quakers and Catholics and Methodists and a few other Anglicans, acting as a heretic or a maverick over against the laws of England, when instruments of mass destruction were found on the streets, at Cruisewatch near Greenham Common, or at RAF Lakenheath, or in places where decisions were taken about the use of such weapons, such as 10 Downing Street (where in those days you could indeed stand or sit on the street outside). This has been a wellspring of my witness, and I remain glad that I stood there, although doing that too brought criticism to me.

Perhaps all these criticisms are justified, perhaps one day I'll grow up enough to understand them and to repudiate my life's journey. Or perhaps not.

In any case mine is far from being the unblemished journey of a saint or a prophet. It's been full of twists and turns, mistakes and apologies, depressions and re-commitments. It has led me from a seat on the road outside 10 Downing Street to (briefly) a seat in the House of Lords, and many would say that sums up a road of contradiction and paradox and compromise and complicity.

But as a result of that journey, I am more and more convinced that if we draw a line that includes us and excludes many others, then Jesus Christ is always on the other side of the line, among the people outside. I want to be there with Him. I have become unashamedly inclusive, for Christ's sake.

And on that road I hope to keep walking, through Christmas and through retirement and on into my own future, as part of the future of this broken and excluding world which needs Jesus so much.

As I prepare to enter another chapter of my life and ministry, I commend the life of looking beyond lines to you all. I hope that you'll walk on that road yourself, unafraid. God is with you. Have a blessed Christmas, and a happy and spirit-filled New Year!

On not being afraid

An Easter piece for Via Media, written in lockdown, on living without anxiety in a frightening world.

People cope with anxiety in different ways. For Christians, the hope and the truth of our faith gives us resources to cope. And the fact that the Coronavirus has struck at this time of the year can be and should be a blessing to those who believe in the resurrection.

However faith in the resurrection is a delicate and fragile thing. It can easily be broken, or at least bent out of shape, by anxiety.

So for example the gift of life in Jesus was received by his disciples as an astonishing and frightening surprise. It's a theme of the gospels that, despite the fact that Jesus spoke about his resurrection before he died, nobody got what he was on about. And so the astonishment and joy of the disciples is tinged, and made more human, by their fear and embarrassment at not having believed what they were so clearly told. Luke's story of the road to Emmaus clearly illustrates the blindness that anxiety can cast over the eyes of people of faith. The two disciples are 'downcast', and so they fail to recognise the living One before their eyes (Luke 24:17).

The risk can be different for those of us who have been Christians for a while. We know about the victory of Jesus. We know that the blessedness of Easter flows from a reversal – light reversing darkness, victory reversing defeat, life reversing death. We are not surprised when Easter comes. We expect life. When these certainties and expectations bump up against anxiety, for example the anxiety caused by a pandemic, the resulting tone can be harsh.

I am not only referring to magical thinking, seen for example in the United States among Christians who continue to meet together, believing that Jesus' blood will see off the virus immediately in their case. Nor am I thinking only of the view that I've seen expressed in the US and in Europe among deeply traditional Catholic Christians – that one consequence of the doctrine of transubstantiation is that the blessed and transformed bread and wine cannot possibly contain, or be a vector for, the virus. These forms of magical thinking are profoundly dangerous, though mercifully pretty rare.

The more common dynamic is beautifully captured by Hilary Ison, drawing in a previous Via Media post from the work of the 'Tragedy and Congregations' project:

> Community responses to disaster typically show a 'heroic phase', full of energy and self-sacrifice, which burns itself out and is followed by a 'disillusionment phase', which may contain much mutual blame and suspicion. Only as the disillusionment phase loses its force can realistic, hopeful re-making take place.

The persistent emphasis of our Lord Jesus was not that his followers should surpass one another in being spectacular in heroism or holiness, but that we should not be afraid. So we are led to an inner place from which we may live a non-anxious life – without heroism, and yet without disillusion, ready to re-make the world. It does not seem particularly glamorous, or exceptional, simply to live our lives without anxiety. But it seems to me that this is our calling at this time. A Church that heeds this command is quietly unafraid; fundamentally marked by the spirit of its Lord. And God knows, to be quietly unafraid is a big ask in these days.

Glimpses of non-anxious living may be seen in many places. As an example from outside the Church of what it might mean, I was challenged and delighted by a recent interview with David Hockney. I've always felt an affinity with this artist, who like me is a Yorkshireman and a Bradford lad. Hockney is a much-beloved artist because of his truthfulness; a gay man who has lived unafraid as he was created, and who for decades has painted the world as he has seen it, carefully and beautifully and accurately. A few days ago he said this:

> We have lost touch with nature rather foolishly as we are a part of it, not outside it. This will in time be over and then what? What have we learned? I am 83 years old, I will die. The cause of death is birth ... the source of art is love.

The faith of Christians is built on Jesus Christ, who saved us on the Cross and who was raised to life at Easter. He it is whom I proclaim. But if I had to express the outworking of that faith in an attitude to the world – to express the non-anxious life – in words that did not mention Jesus, I could do a good deal worse than those words of Hockney.

And if I ever reach the age of 83, I hope that this will be my approach. That this approach, built on the faith in Jesus that I have received as a gift, will issue in a non-anxious life. That I might be truthful, and speak simply, and not fear death, and see love at the root of things.

And as we move into Eastertide, and as the number of cases of the virus and the number of deaths continues to rise, I hope that I may resist anxiety as my Lord commanded me to do, and that I may live in hope, and may love my neighbour in ways that will help them first. In that spirit I wish you all a blessed Easter. Not necessarily a happy one, not for so many of us; no. But in the faith of Christ a blessed one nonetheless; one in which we may live, unafraid, in the One who loves us.

On Fr Bill

A Via Media reflection, paying tribute to another guy who lived in stillness of heart and on the edge of things, and whose witness spoke to me of Christ.

In 1982 I moved to west London to minister as a University chaplain there. I had been ordained for three years. The West London Chaplaincy was a wonderful, creative outfit; it had been set up a generation before by Ivor Smith-Cameron and had no place of its own, being built around small groups meeting weekly in halls, departments and community houses. There were about 60 of these groups each week. The work was very rewarding. Intellectually demanding certainly, but it was also lovely to minister alongside Christian students; men and women whose sense of identity, and Christian calling, grew as they learned from one another.

It was at this time, as a young priest wanting to make sense of my life and of ministry, that I connected with the late, great Bill Kirkpatrick, who became my spiritual director. Fr Bill lived in a basement flat in Earl's Court, from where he opened his heart to the community through 'Reaching Out', his ministry of presence and listening and love. He had converted a coal cellar, under the Inner Ring Road, into a chapel, with plain whitewashed walls and (for a place that shook whenever a lorry rolled over its roof) an extraordinary quietness and peace.

Fr Bill was an intense presence. His listening released truth in the people he met. He wore a wooden holding cross around his neck. He made a great cup of tea. At the end of every session he would say 'Thanks for sharing', and I'd go and pray in that coal cellar and then walk up to Earl's Court tube station feeling that I'd been heard and understood, and feeling that life was richer than I had known before.

I was not the only one to receive wisdom from Bill, whose ministry was widespread and deeply respected. (For example Colin

Coward has written movingly of his own connection with him.)[109] But in the years I knew him, Bill's ministry took on one focus in particular, because of where he was and who he was. For Bill was a gay partnered man living in Earl's Court, and these were the years of what was then a mystery illness that devastated and further marginalised the gay community in London, as in so many other cities; the early years of AIDS/HIV.

And so, more and more, Bill's life was spent accompanying people in their journey of illness and too often of death and bereavement. He brought a listening ear and the openness and love of Christ to people in fear and desperate need, people who saw all too little of that openness and love in communities of Christians that told them nothing more than that they were sinners, and passed by on the other side when they fell ill.

I write this partly to give honour to Fr Bill, who died three years ago this month and whose radical mission and radical ministry deserves to be celebrated at any time. But I write it in particular now because those years have been dramatised and recaptured by Russell T. Davies in his TV series *It's a Sin*.[110]

The series follows a group of young people, mostly gay men, as the adventure of their adult lives begins in the 1980s. We are with them as they find themselves, and then find themselves under a terrible shadow. It's truthful, honest, unsparing about the consequences of unknowing and unbridled promiscuity in a community that was still finding out how to live wisely in a world where love was not forbidden. It also remembers energy and laughter and joy and friendship and care and life, sustained even in the face of fear and illness and death.

It is resonant. Gay friends of mine have been triggered by it this week, remembering people they loved and lost in those years, remembering their own experience of living in the shadows, still hearing the homophobic echoes in their lives today. *It's a Sin* is a title with a lot of resonance – it references the Pet Shop Boys' song of course, but wherever did Chris and Neil get the idea for such a title or for such a lyric?

Neil Tennant has said his song 'was intended as a camp joke and it wasn't something I consciously took very seriously'. But he went on: 'Sometimes I wonder if there was more to it than I thought at the time …'[111]

Well, yes, you do wonder. Thirty years later, poor little talkative Christianity continues to chatter along. The churches' conversations on love and faith, which so many are still pleased to call 'debates', will continue for a good while yet. Human lives will continue to be pressed like flowers between the covers of one book or another.

For myself, I love the body of Christ and I believe Jesus was serious when he asked his Father that we might all be one. So I will continue to do my best to take part in these conversations. In them I will do my best to advocate for love and marriage for all, in the persistent hope that Christ's body may move forward together, may indeed be one, in love.

But when from time to time all this talking gets too much and I tiptoe out of the room in search of the God of love, when I want to follow Jesus Christ onto the street, I'm going to remember Fr Bill Kirkpatrick – a partnered gay man with a ministry on the edge of the church to people on the edge of the world, a man who reached out.

And I'll remember a coal cellar under the London streets, and place of contemplation and silence as the cars roar overhead. And a priest with a ministry of 'hearing through listening', a ministry of unfailing presence, a ministry of encouragement for so many including me, most of all a ministry of listening to his people where his people were – listening in the hubbub of the Coleherne pub, listening on the street, listening on the ward, listening by the grave. And alongside all this a ministry of resourcing and writing[112] – about prayer, about AIDS, about death, and in everything he wrote, about life.

Thanks for sharing, Bill. Remembering you I'll remember that a self-absorbed, censorious and condemning Christianity need not have the last word – it will indeed never have the last word, because the last word is life beyond death.[113]

On finding a place to stand

This final Via Media fragment is based on a piece about street wisdom, in the light of the Extinction Rebellion movement.

Last Thursday I stood with a number of colleagues, lay and ordained, as part of the Christian Climate Action contribution to the Extinction Rebellion protests in London. We read from the book of Revelation in Trafalgar Square, standing in front of the National Gallery, surrounded by people of all faiths and none who were taking their stand together to form part of this extraordinary non-violent direct action movement.

I was not at risk of arrest on that day. Some of my ordained colleagues there had been arrested the previous day, and a great many Christians have been arrested before and since, just a few of the 2600+ people (at the time of writing) who have taken their protest to the point of loss of liberty. Without violence they break the law and they face the music. And who are we to judge?

On the way to Trafalgar Square I passed Downing Street and Admiralty Arch, two of the several places where I myself had been arrested in the 1980s, so forty years ago. At that time it was my great privilege to be a national co-chair of Christian CND, and to have been able to take a stand within the wide rainbow of non-violent advocacy which wanted to see nuclear weapons banned, within the still wider rainbow made up of people who find themselves on the street because they want to change the world for the better in any way. That was around the time of the 'Church and the Bomb' report. I spent time lobbying the General Synod and arguing with bishops, and I spent time on the street, and time in the cells at Cannon Row police station. All that advocacy felt like one seamless thing to me.

And the arguments used against Extinction Rebellion on that occasion were also familiar to me, since the same things had been said to me whenever I sat in the road, or chained myself to railings, or prayed persistently outside a US base, or otherwise took action all those years ago. 'Isn't this just ridiculous middle-class posturing?' 'Aren't you just messing about?' 'Do you really think that these protests will change policy – will change anything at all?'

All these are sensible questions, but they miss the point. The point is that non-violent advocacy is a wide, wide rainbow, and each colour in it has its place, and it would be foolish to assume that no part of it makes or will make a difference. It's a matter of diversity, as St Paul understood very well when he spoke of the body and its different parts.

The advocacy of Mahatma Gandhi or of Dr Martin Luther King took its place within this diverse, non-violent, world-changing rainbow. Within the rainbow some will work quietly and unobtrusively to influence political and other leaders with facts, evidence, scholarship, quiet wisdom, nuance. Others will follow the advice of an editor of the *Economist*: 'Simplify, then exaggerate', crafting messages which motivate the heart and lead people to take a stand, and proclaiming them clearly and very loudly.

In the case of Extinction Rebellion the messages and demands are suitably loud and clear:[114]

- Tell the truth (and declare a climate emergency)
- Act now (and move to net-zero greenhouse gas emissions by 2025)
- Go beyond politics (and establish a citizens' assembly to focus the practical steps).

The details of these demands are of course open to debate, and so are some of the tactical choices made about where and how to protest and what to disrupt. But when it comes to the future of the planet the rainbow of advocacy needs Extinction Rebellion, just as it needs Greta Thunberg and the school strikes. The urgency of the climate crisis means that nuanced debate between sophisticated grown-ups is not enough.

All this is personal. It bears in on each one of us, as Bishop Rowan Williams knows. Writing in the afterword to the XR manual *This Is Not A Drill*,[115] he has this to say:

> To put it very directly: it is worth changing our habits of consumption, the default settings for our lifestyle, the various

kinds of denial and evasion of bodily reality that suit us, the fantasies of limitless growth and control, simply because there are healthy and unhealthy ways of living in this universe.

To go on determinedly playing the trumpet in a string quartet is a recipe for frustration and collapse and conflict. There are ways of learning to live better, to make peace with the world. Learn them anyway: they will limit the disease and destruction; they may even be seeds for a future we can't imagine ...

It just might work.

And as a person of faith he says:

In the Book of Proverbs, in the Hebrew Scriptures, the divine wisdom is described as 'filled with delight' at the entire world which flows from that wisdom. For me as a religious believer, the denial or corruption of that delight is like spitting in the face of the life-giving Word who is to be met in all things and all people ...

And he ends by saying:

Anger, love and joy may sound like odd bedfellows, but these are the seeds of a future that will offer life – not success, but life.

So what? Well, with all this in mind, there is a question for you who are reading this. On this matter – the future of the planet – and indeed on any other matter of justice and peace, will you take your stand within the rainbow of non-violent advocacy? And if you will, where will be the right place, the best place, for you yourself to stand?

Of course some approaches stand outside any non-violent advocacy rainbow. On one side is the assumption that no advocacy is necessary at all, or perhaps that advocating is so naïve as to be pointless, or perhaps that we can't be bothered – that other people will engage with it and so we won't have to. And on the other side, the assumption that only violence will change things, or that if we feel we must break the law, then having broken the law, no consequences should or must be faced.

Neither of these approaches was taken by Mahatma Gandhi, or by Dr King. As they engaged with the issues of justice that lay before them, each one understood the spectrum of advocacy and operated across it; at times pragmatic, at times prophetic. Jesus too spoke highly of the law and also acted in ways that challenged it, reaching out to the excluded. In those words of the Lutheran Gordon Lathrop that so often speak to my own heart, '…we are speaking of the biblical, historic Christ who eats with sinners and outsiders, who is made a curse and sin itself for us, who justifies the ungodly, and who is himself the hole in any system'.

Jesus lived with urgency, for the times were urgent. The times for us too are urgent, as indeed they have always been.

So if you're a Christian, in matters of the future of the planet, in all matters of justice and peace, will you open the door to the heart, and there listen for the voice of the triune God who loves you, the voice of the Holy Spirit at the core of you who comforts and provokes you? Will you let the door swing onto the street, and take your stand within the rainbow of non-violent advocacy? And if you take your stand, will you stand there? And if not now, when?

On having sex on the brain

A keynote address given at the online conference of MoSAIC (the Movement of Supporting Anglicans for an Inclusive Church) in June 2021. MoSAIC described itself as 'a coalition bringing together campaigns on issues such as race, ability, sexuality, gender, and gender identity'.

The original text of this one landed me in hot water, because some conservative brothers and sisters were offended by what they saw as personal attacks on their views and their integrity (for example I had described the theologically conservative community as 'always looking for a new ditch to die in'). I apologised for this language, which was indeed unthinking and gratuitous (especially in the light of the final story in the piece about Ruth Bader Ginsburg) and shortened the text slightly. The inoffensive version follows.

First of all let me thank you for the invitation and for the privilege of speaking to you today. It's great to be with a group of people on a journey who are learning as they go and reflecting truth to one another, as the process of this conference has shown.

The MoSAIC network is a valuable and indeed necessary part of the Church, because inclusion is a Gospel matter. Inclusion speaks of love, and inclusion is seamless.

I believe that your agenda will align the Church more closely with the life and values of Jesus. It speaks of love and of the God of love, and it is also the world's agenda – no matter what the culture warriors might shout, no matter how many people are chanting now that the things that matter to us as 'woke'. In the words of Dr King, quoting Theodore Parker a century before, the arc of the moral universe is long, but it bends towards justice.

Being called woke has become an insult, but it is better than being asleep, and MoSAIC is a movement of wakefulness. We have all seen the growth, or re-growth, of anti-liberal philosophies in the West, and 2016 was a watershed year. For those committed to inclusion there is a work to do within and beyond the Church. And yet, in the midst of all that contention, the agenda of inclusion remains the world's agenda, and remains worth advocating, and struggling for, so that wakefulness may be the mark of God's people who are called to watch.

In the mid to late 1960s the World Council of Churches developed an understanding of mission. The soundbite that summed up their understanding was this: 'Let the world set the agenda'.

For many of us in the Church, the world setting the agenda seems so faithless, because God should come first, and anyway we know we're right. How dare people who are not believers presume to tell us when and how the way we live is offensive or damaging?

But the fact is that in the areas we've been addressing – increasingly in the area of racial justice and disability justice, and overwhelmingly in this area of sexuality, as well of course as in the area of secrecy and abuse, the arc of the moral universe keeps on bending towards justice. Look at our football team, kneeling in the face of the boos of the sleepwalkers so as to advocate for justice. The world beyond the church has set the moral agenda, and those who kneel with our footballers, or who see no difference between attending the marriage of their gay or their straight friends or work colleagues, find the community of faith to be wanting and indeed increasingly offensive. Nowhere is that more true than in the area of human sexuality.

It was Malcolm Muggeridge in the mid-1960s who famously said: 'It has to be admitted that we English have sex on the brain, which is a very unsatisfactory place to have it'. I won't go into Muggeridge's own rather complicated journey except to say that here, he knew what he was talking about.

And he was right. We English, and certainly we in the Church of England, have sex on the brain, which is a very unsatisfactory place to have it.

You don't get to choose your agendas, and you don't get to hide your least favourite agenda by covering it with lots of other justice cards. Inclusion is seamless. And in our generation sexuality is the agenda that the church would so love to move on from but which, inconveniently, the culture of the West and of this country uses as a touchstone for us.

On many occasions in the past, particular issues have been seen as deal-breakers for the unity of the Church. Divorce, contraception, the place of women in ministry – all these differences are now held within the Church's unity, though each of them was the last ditch in its time. And now in our generation sexuality in general, and same-sex relationships in particular, have come to be seen by some as the line that somehow God has always wanted us to draw in the sand.

But in fact the agenda of same-sex love and faithfulness and the blessing of its expression has been given to us, and certainly to me, by the world – the world which God so loved. My kids' generation, and the generations younger than my kids which include now the youngest generation of the ordained, are bewildered and amazed that we can't seem to stop having sex on the brain.

The mildly progressive and inclusive things that I myself have said and written on all this have been received with extraordinary generosity and gratitude by my kids' friends and by the LGBT+ community in the Liverpool region and beyond, and although I never asked for this agenda before I came to Liverpool, I am glad to have inhabited that space now. As I grow older and the arc of my own ministry draws close to its end, I am glad to be able to speak wholeheartedly for a vision of Christian community that commends itself to people who honour love where it is to be found, and who want to celebrate it.

We English have sex on the brain, which is a very unsatisfactory place to have it. We also have religion on the brain, and that's no better. Having sex or religion on the brain is an awful place to have it. Few approaches have been used to crush dissent or to enforce loneliness more than the approach that says 'Let's do some more theology on this. Scholars agree ...'. But God made more than minds, and God is bigger than conceptual arguments. As St Gregory of Nyssa said back in the fourth century: 'Concepts create idols of God, of whom only wonder can tell us anything.'

So MoSAIC is a network that can help the Church to learn from its incarnate Lord and from the beauty of the body. Some of you may have heard me tell this story before, but ever since I heard it from my mentor Bishop Peter Selby, it has lived in me as a piece of Gospel truth. At the height of the AIDS crisis the Bishop of California was visited by a group of church people who demanded that he condemn what some people still call 'the gay lifestyle'. The bishop replied, 'God took the risk of becoming a human being. Why can't you?'

The Incarnation goes beyond the life of the mind, and the balanced intellectual 'debates' which educated western men in particular love so much, the clear teaching that some see as all that matters, the glittering arguments of the brain, are put in their place by the mystery of the body.

Sex partakes of the mystery of the body, and sex with its surrenders and its vulnerabilities and its comedies and its glory is a deep and profound mystery. That's why having it on the brain is a very unsatisfactory place to have it. I have used the word 'debates' and the conversations that are ongoing around 'Living in Love and Faith' are still described that way by some as 'debates', as though we were living in the Oxford Union, as though real people's lives can be picked over remotely and intellectually without damage.

They can't. People's love is a mystery and their body is made by God as a mystery, and people are afraid of mysteries, and so the body is feared by those for whom the tidy mind matters most. The mystery of people's sexuality, the untidy fact that people live their lives to quirky templates, all this is implicit in the incarnation, and it makes holiness complicated and even messy – certainly messier than debate.

As Einstein said in a scientific context, 'Everything should be made as simple as possible, but not simpler'. People grow up and fall in love and their mysterious bodies lead them to love as they love, and they will love whom they love, and no amount of harrumphing is going to change that.

Of course desire itself is also a mystery. Desire is a driver and a road to holiness, or to dissipation, and Christianity has much to say about the need to move to holiness and to love, to be disciplined lovers, and to forgive one another, and to shun the selfish abuse of love.

But desire runs on the road of the body, and the body's road runs mysteriously. That's what causes fear, and fear brings with it a fog. And so people assume norms and impose norms and discipline those who differ, even though they are seeking to take the desires they have been given and to direct them well. And this is simply wrong. It's wrong.

Fear of sex stems from fear of the body, not fear of desire. And as Rowan Williams said in *The Body's Grace* in 1989, 'there would be less need for LGCM and kindred organisations [including of course MoSAIC today] if sex were not alarming to so many'.

For those of us who are inclusive Christians, the risk of becoming a human being is always a risk worth taking, since Jesus went that way. And that people should live fully into who they were made to be is a delight and not a problem.

Anyway, because we still have sex on the brain in England, MoSAIC has a particular job of advocacy to do if sexuality is to be included in the basket of inclusion. No one will say, at least not explicitly, that issues of racial justice, or of disability discrimination, should in principle be overshadowed by our Christian faith or are in some way in conflict with the rights of Christian people to practice their religion.

But sexuality is in a different place, and so we need to advocate, and you yourselves need, as individuals and as an organisation, to take your place in the family of advocates and on the spectrum of advocacy.

That spectrum is wide. It includes some whose very lives are under the microscope and indeed at risk from personal and institutional homophobia and transphobia and whose anger is white-hot. We need those voices. It includes people who have been awakened to the need for greater justice because members of their family or people they know are living loves of evident holiness in same-sex or trans contexts. We need those voices. It includes moderate people who see the way society is moving and who can't see a problem with that; we need those voices. It includes corporate bodies, such as in this sector One Body One Faith, or Changing Attitude or Equal or Open Table, or the Ozanne Foundation with which I'm linked myself, or wider-scoped advocates such as Inclusive Church or MoSAIC; and we need all those voices. And the result of wholehearted advocacy by lots of people with a wide spectrum of voices and thoughts and lived examples will be change, I hope and pray.

The arc of my own ministry is drawing near its end; I was ordained 42 years ago and I'm in my 68th year. But I want to take my place on that spectrum of advocacy, just as you do.

What do I want to see? I want to see a Church that is no longer institutionally racist. I want to see a Church where people with physical or mental or emotional disability are honoured and accommodated and learned from and loved, and whose love is received as a gift.

In the area of sexuality and relationships I want to see the road which runs through Living in Love and Faith come to a good destination. The LLF process has clarified my own thinking.

I want to see a gender-neutral marriage canon, such as they have in the Episcopal Church or in the Scottish Episcopal Church. And as a necessary but not sufficient first step, I want to see conscientious freedom for the Church's ministers and local leaders to honour, recognise and, yes indeed, to bless same-sex unions whether civil partnerships or civil marriages.

I want to see an abolition of the foolishness that sees the call to ordained ministry as a call to a state morally higher than that of the baptised, as though baptism called us to a lesser holiness. I want to see an end to LGBTQ+ people hiding who they are for fear of being exposed to conversion therapy or to being forbidden to minister in churches. I want to see an end to the inquisition of ordinands about their private lives.

I want to see all this before I die. These things must be done and I hope and believe that LLF will awaken the church and open the door to them.

And I do want us to remain one church, and within that church for example I want to see the conscientious rights of conservative people preserved for them.

But I don't want any longer to see the conscientious rights of progressive people, who believe the truth of the Archbishops of Canterbury and York when they ask for a radical NEW Christian inclusion, I don't want to see their consciences ignored and explained away and overridden, or their freedom delayed in the name of 'doing more theology'.

I want to see a church where those rights are liberated so that people's love can be blessed. And in the end I want to see a gender-neutral marriage canon so that the goods and joys of marriage can be extended to all and fenced around no longer.

In these fractious and increasingly authoritarian days, these post-truth days, I want to see a church that proclaims that love is love and the recognises and affirmed and blesses love where it sees it. I want to see a church that learns from the poor in spirit and the broken and the oppressed and the hungry and the grieving, just as Jesus said.

Inclusion is seamless, and I think MoSAIC understands that. So I want to see more people like you, and to encourage you, and to share with you the task of holding these values before the Church, and before the electors to the General Synod, and in the end before the world.

In my kitchen there's a tea towel from the Radical Tea Towel Company. It has a picture of the great US jurist Ruth Bader Ginsburg, and it has these words of hers: 'Fight for the things that you care about. But do it in a way that will lead others to join you.' Take your place with courage on the spectrum of advocacy, friends, and help to establish the coalition that sees the arc of the moral universe bend towards justice.

Thank you for the privilege of sharing with you.

On conversion therapy

A General Synod speech, July 2017.

I pay tribute again here to Jayne Ozanne, who proposed the original motion on Conversion Therapy, giving the General Synod the rare opportunity to speak clearly in a progressive cause. And Synod did.

The amended motion was as follows:

'That this Synod: – endorse the Memorandum of Understanding on Conversion Therapy in the UK of November 2015, signed by The Royal College of Psychiatrists and others, that the practice of gay conversion therapy has no place in the modern world, is unethical, potentially harmful and not supported by evidence; – call upon the Church to be sensitive to, and to listen to, contemporary expressions of gender identity; – and call on the government to ban the practice of Conversion Therapy.'

The Synod approved this motion overwhelmingly. The votes in the House of Bishops were 36 for and one against, with no abstentions. In the House of Clergy 135 backed the motion with 25 against and 13 abstentions. In the House of Laity 127 supported the motion with 48 opposing and 13 abstentions.

Here's my own speech, which I tried to make as plain as I could.

As the world listens to us the world needs to hear us say that LGBTI+ orientation and identity is not a crime. LGBTI+ orientation and identity is not a sickness. And LGBTI+ orientation and identity is not a sin.

We must distinguish between an ascetic and a therapeutic approach. In the Church we are certainly called to help one another to conform lives to Jesus Christ and to live lives of holiness, but we do not need to engage people in healing therapy if they are not sick.

We disagree about the way forward for LGBTI+ people who want to live in holiness. Some here will insist that celibacy is the only way. Others here – including me – want to offer the choice of celibacy or faithful, permanent, stable relationship to LGBTI+ people just as it is routinely offered to heterosexual and cisgender people in our Church. But these disagreements are not at issue today.

What matters here is that a therapeutic model is not appropriate if LGBTI+ orientation and identity is not a sickness. And if the Church suggests that really, actually it is, then our many statements opposing homophobia are void, and the world will think that in fact we really do believe LGBTI+ people to be second-class humans no matter how they behave; and this is not acceptable to me and I hope not to this Synod. That's why I will vote for this motion.

Later this month at home we will celebrate Liverpool Pride, with which I am proud and privileged to be associated. We celebrate Pride later than most places because of the death of Michael Causer, an 18-year-old gay man who died in August 2008 following a brutal homophobic attack.

Michael did not die because he was sick or sinful or because he had committed a crime. He died because he was hated, in a culture where that hate was ignored or avoided or tolerated or fed; and we the Church must seize every opportunity to say that we will not have a culture in which such hate can find purchase.

And to say that all people need help to live lives of holiness, however they interpret that; but that no one needs to be ashamed of or cured of their orientation or identity, and that it is spiritually abusive to suggest that they do.

I exhort Synod to vote for this motion.

On being an ally

Another opportunity to thank someone, this time Steve Chalke, the founder of the Oasis movement. In 2018 Oasis called a conference, 'The Gender Agenda', on the pastoral richness of working with trans people (Steve has also written a book with this title). Again, in the years since this piece was written the trans community has found itself increasingly scapegoated and even demonised, used as a reason for all kinds of illiberalism.

I honour Steve for calling this conference and for writing the book that accompanied it, and for all the other pieces of pastoral care and courageous advocacy that have comprised his significant and fruitful ministry.

I'm very grateful to Steve for the invitation to speak this morning, and grateful to you all for the welcome. It's an honour to be here and to stand with the aims of this conference.

I've been asked to talk about 'The Role of Allies in Creating Trans Justice'. I want to begin by trying to brush aside a misunderstanding about being an ally.

The misunderstanding I mean is a power idea. It's the idea that allies are people who have their lives together and who have decided to help some group or other of poor people whose lives are fragmented by confusion or by social pressure and who need champions who will fight for them.

I call it a power idea because it produces so-called allies who are actually in charge, dispensing bounty and wisdom from the place of power. Anyway that's certainly not how I see what being an ally should be.

One dictionary definition of 'ally' is to 'combine or unite … with (another) for mutual benefit'. I like that definition.

I'm a 67 year old cis straight white man with a job in the

church that gives me a platform, and so I'm bathed in the privilege that blinkers and that so easily puffs up. And I want to be an ally in creating justice because if people – today trans people, or more widely LGBT+ people, or black people, or working class people – if people are not free then I'm not free.

Shon Faye has a recent book out, which ironically is called *The Transgender Issue*. I say ironically because in it she writes: 'We [trans people] are not an 'issue' to be debated and derided. We are symbols of hope for non-trans people too, who see in our lives the possibility of living more fully and freely.'

I want to be an ally, but I know that you don't get to call yourself an ally. It's for the community on the edge of things to bestow the title if they feel you should have it. So whether I am an ally is not for me to say – but I want to be one.

I want to stand as an ally because I believe that I need to lose the blinkers of my privilege and to wake up, and to work to begin to understand the experience of my allies – so that I myself may be free and may receive life and joy from the place where God is to be found, that is from the edge of things. In short I want and need to be an ally for my friends, but also for my soul's health.

In preparation for this session I contacted four people I know, trans or non-binary people, for advice. One of the themes of that advice was that I should recognise my own transphobia and seek healing from it.

That's where my walk as an ally begins. I live with my unconscious bias, and I sleepwalk often, and I need to wake up. I don't believe it's the responsibility of my trans friends to heal my transphobia, but I do want to attempt the work of healing so that I can be a better ally because a freer person.

I believe allies can do some helpful work around clearing space, and making space, and then relinquishing space. Because of who I am or what do, I may have access to a space that I can clear, or help to build, or establish – so that people on the edge of things may come into that space with confidence.

That may be particularly necessary when the space is contended, and the space is fiercely contended for trans people at the moment – contended among other ways through old controversies in my own Christian faith community, and by new controversies with the so-called gender-critical community.

I'm not called to be a 'champion' as if my interventions might replace the real lives of real people. People who are already fully human and who are becoming more fully human in this struggle, their humanity does not need me to affirm it. God affirms it.

Sometimes you may hear rhetoric around the role of people with a platform, like bishops and others, that goes like this: we are there to speak as a voice for the voiceless. I don't find that language at all helpful.

But sometimes it is possible for allies to clear a space, and to share a platform, and then to leave the platform to those who can perfectly well speak for themselves, and whose voice will persuade and convict and transform the conversation if only people will hear it.

To clear space and build a platform and then step aside is part of the ally's role, I think. Trans people are people, and in the end it is understanding the lived experience of human beings that will change the world.

This is not to say that being an ally is some sort of neutral act that doesn't require courage. The trans space in particular is one where disagreements can be violent and where people take what they think is the truth and use it like a blade to hurt and to wound people. As my father used to say: 'the truth is a sharp sword; you can kill more than falsehood with it'. In such a world, as the Jesuit peace protestor the late Fr Dan Berrigan used to say, it helps if you 'know where you stand, and stand there'.

Too often, in the church and elsewhere, the pressure is on for leaders to act as if everything was an abstract, and to treat the real lives of real people like counters in a game or like examples in an Oxford Union debate. I don't believe that's right. As a Christian I don't believe that Jesus led that way.

So. Trans men are men. Trans women are women. Non-binary people are people. My allyship starts there, and I'll try to say it clearly. And if that exposes me to a tiny fraction of the hostility that so many of you must face daily, then I will readily accept that as a consequence.

I don't have all the answers in these controversies. I'm a cis man and so I need to learn from the experience and from the lives of others, including gender-critical people. But meanwhile justice is not a zero-sum game, and justice for trans and non-binary people is not negotiable. Trans men are men. Trans women are women. Non-binary people are people. I'm starting there.

I said earlier that I asked a few colleagues and friends for advice on how to be an ally in creating trans justice, and I asked them too to reflect on my own record as someone who tries to be an ally. I'm very grateful to all four of them for taking the trouble to engage. Here are some of the things they said.

- All of them wanted to make clear their conviction that generalising experience is a foolish and indeed hurtful thing. Everyone is different, and honouring difference is the compass for our advocacy. As one of my conversation partners said: 'When you've heard one trans story, you've done precisely that'.
- When it comes to raising consciousness, I was told it helps not to take over conversations but to listen, It's not the responsibility of trans people to educate cis people but it is the responsibility of cis people to understand and to read, speak and listen so as to understand better.
- Someone said: 'Do your own research! There are lots of resources out there about trans identities and trans culture, and doing your own research takes the onus off your local friendly trans person to explain everything all the time.'
- Someone said: 'Point away from yourself and don't assume that your job is to be a voice for the voiceless'.
- I was reminded that this is a new time, and so for example mistakes in using pronouns and not avoiding deadnames are easily made. As one of my conversation partners, a young person, said: 'If you do make mistakes, just apologise quickly and move on. Don't make a big deal out of it, but don't ignore it either.'
- And they said, 'Normalise asking for pronouns, and giving your own. When you meet someone, try telling them which pronouns you use, and give them space to respond if they want'.
- And they said: 'Help us fight for our rights. Trans rights in the UK are under attack from transphobic hate groups, and the fight to be recognised and respected is long and hard. Protest with us, fight alongside us, donate to trans rights causes, and help us in whatever way you can.'
- A married person encouraged me to support the spouses of married trans people and to listen carefully there and not make assumptions. In particular I'm advised not to assume trauma in a relationship if trauma is not present. The same thing applies

to assuming trauma in a person who is transitioning, when the reality may very well be that the transitioning is precisely a healing from trauma.
- And finally another person looked at all this complicated scene and then they quoted scripture and reminded me that in the Bible it says: 'God walks in the cool of the day'.

There's a spiritual discipline in wanting to be an ally. For people of faith it involves prayer, and silence, and courage.

There's a US cowboy saying that President Lyndon Johnson had on his wall: 'If you're talking, you ain't learning'. One of my conversation partners said that allies sometimes need to be big, and to have broad backs, loud mouths, big ears, strong hands. All of that helps, but big ears helps most. So the role of allies in creating trans justice begins and ends in listening.

God walks in the cool of the day. Bodies are mysterious, and desire is mysterious, and that makes people anxious, and so there's too much of the heat of the day, too much of people trying to force and cookie-cut one another to fit their own ideas of how the world should be.

But the world is as it is. And in that world I want to be a good ally. And so I'll be as loud and broad and strong as I can, so that I can be helpful, and be free with the free, so that I can work to see trans and non-binary people flourish in our schools and our faith communities and our society.

But for me, and especially for me as a person of faith, it begins and ends in listening to the people who are pushed to the edge, the people who matter most. That's what I aim to do, and that's how I shall myself become more free, and more human.

Thank you.

On ecumenism

Some bits of this final piece, especially the section called 'Sweat', are a bit grainy and detailed. I hope the sections called 'Blood' and 'Tears' are more immediately accessible. But I wanted to include the whole thing because ecumenism has been so important to me, and it seems less worthy of sweat for many Christians in this season.

In Liverpool we had an annual lecture in memory of a previous bishop, Stuart Blanch, who went on in his day to become Archbishop of York. This, then, is the Blanch Memorial Lecture for 2015. In it I tell the story of Roland Walls, another hero of mine.

When I visited his tiny community in Scotland on retreat, he and I went for a walk together and, as they used to do in the Egyptian desert all those years ago, I asked him for 'a word, that I might live'. He thought for a moment and then 'Bumble', he said. 'Bumble more as you go along'. I've been trying to do so ever since. In many ways this might be a word for the whole driven Church in our generation.

Anyway, here's the Blanch Lecture 2015.

Ecumenism: blood, sweat and tears

I'm very grateful to the Trustees for the invitation to deliver this lecture here at Hope in memory of Archbishop Stuart Blanch. Grateful, too, to Guy Elsmore for suggesting ecumenism as the field of enquiry. As I stand here in Archbishop Stuart's name and in the role which he fulfilled in the city in so distinguished a manner,

I'm aware that in the ecumenical endeavour, as in so many of the emphases of our Diocese, he was a pioneer. This is also, perhaps even more, true of his wife Brenda, with whom Stuart conducted a steady conversation about the relationship between the churches as their letters record, and who in 1944 wrote 'More and more God seems to be training me to see the futility of all these divisions in the church, that in Christ we are not divided. I often feel that I should be a lot happier in a remote mission field where services were simple praise etc. I'm so tired of complicated liturgy, convention, unreality.' This in 1944 – we're not told what she thought of all that in Stuart's years as a bishop …

Brenda also wrote in the same year: 'It is a pity that the fellowship of the Nonconformists and the sense of worship that the C of E has cannot be combined, isn't it? Neither is complete and satisfying without the other.'

This early example of so-called 'receptive ecumenism' – the idea that we come together with our deficits and needs, rather than our riches, at the top of our minds, in a spirit of reception rather than proclamation – is one of many examples in Dick Williams' biography, of Brenda's keeping the need of the unity of the churches before Stuart – though he himself had a lively awareness of the matter also, and made ecumenism a reality in his parish ministry, as his anonymous contribution to 'The Lee Abbey Story' in 1956 indicates. There he said: 'Where new life has come to a parish it has led to a remarkable degree of co-operation between the different Christian bodies in the place'.

So in following Archbishop Stuart I am treading in the footsteps of a pioneer and an apostle of unity, on whose foundations in Liverpool the great work of Bishop Sheppard and Archbishop Worlock, and the extension of that work by Bishop James and Archbishop Patrick, were constructed.

The conversations, in writing and no doubt much more in the quietness of the home, between Brenda Blanch as an instinctive ecumenist and Stuart Blanch as a builder of coalition – these conversations remind us that like most things in the life of faith, the ecumenical endeavour is one of emotional commitment and human motivation far more than it is one of cool and considered thought alone. It reminds us in short that people are complicated, and that their experience and formation brings that complication to everything they do and to this endeavour not least.

You'll see from the title that I hope to approach my subject of enquiry through three doors, which I've called blood, sweat and tears. But before I go to those doors, let me begin with a story which some here will have heard before, a favourite story of mine, about I man I knew and revered as a spiritual teacher, which hints at something of the depth and complexity of human motivation. Alongside its incidental charm, I tell this story to set the ecumenical endeavour in the widest possible context – the context of what makes each of us tick, and of how the decisions that change our lives can sometimes be made. And I hope that the moral of the story, if it can be seen in that way, will become clear as I complement it with another story about this same man towards the end of my lecture.

Motivations and reasons

Roland Walls was a successful Anglican priest, a Canon of Sheffield, where he had been crafting and delivering creative training for Anglican clergy, close to what today we would call mixed-mode training, which tried hard to relate the orthodox Gospel to England as it actually is. He had explored a monastic vocation with the Taizé community and he was still unsure what God wanted him to do and to be. He had no shortage of options. Indeed he had received an offer to be an Oxford College chaplain and another offer to become Master of the Royal Foundation of St Katherine in Limehouse. Each of these would have spoken of 'success' and would have kept his feet on the ladder of church preferment. But then alongside these he was offered a tiny and obscure job in the Scottish Episcopal Church, non-stipended, looking after a chapel in a small village in Midlothian. He went to visit, and then on his way home had to decide what to do. He takes up the story:

> I went on that lovely train from Waverley through Carlisle. When I got to Leeds city station I remember I was praying to the Lord, and I was getting mad at him, and I was saying 'Now Lord, I don't know what you're doing' – because I was 45 – and I said, 'Lord, you've got me where you want me because I will do what you say as long as you make it perfectly clear to me

what it is. I really don't mind what I do of all these things but I will do anything as long as you make it clear; so jolly well get on with it.' That was the kind of prayer I was saying, when all of a sudden, coming out of Leeds the other way was a big coal train, all of twenty trucks, and on the back, on the guard's van, it had a big notice, red letters, and it said, 'RETURN EMPTY TO SCOTLAND'. The word EMPTY was underlined. I said, 'Right, Lord'. This event, on my return from seeing this highly unpromising little chapel, is the only reason we're at Roslin.

And he stayed in Scotland as a monk and a teacher for the rest of his long life, dying there last year at the age of 95. I'll return later to Roland Walls when I speak of his contribution to what I've called the ecumenism of tears. For now let him stand as a patron of this enquiry, a reminder that we do what we do for all sorts of reasons, and we explain them to ourselves afterwards in all sorts of ways.

The seasons of ecumenism

I was born in 1953 in Bradford, Yorkshire. My parents were devout Anglicans and fully involved in their local parish church, as I was also during my childhood.

For the first ten years of my life the ecumenical climate was wintry. In the year of my birth Stuart Blanch as Vicar of Eynsham was forging those links with other denominations which were referred to in the Lee Abbey book mentioned a moment ago. But he was by no means typical. More commonly the Church of England luxuriated in its role as the default religious option for nominal believers. The Roman Catholic Church remained a fortress from which it was not even permissible to pray the Lord's Prayer with other Christians or to enter their places of worship. Sectarianism, here in Liverpool as in so many places, was a hard and sometimes a violent reality. The union schemes of the churches in South India produced severe strain in the counsels of the Church of England. At theological college I received my liturgical education at the hands of a man who had left the C of E over the South India scheme, eventually finding his home in the Orthodox church. Meanwhile the free churches went each in their own way.

Then, relatively suddenly, in the 1960s winter gave way to the spring. The second Vatican Council, called by Pope John XXIII in 1963, brought a fresh approach to that Communion, not least in its decree on ecumenism, Unitatis Redintegratio, passed by a vote of 2,137 to 11 of the bishops assembled and promulgated by Pope Paul VI on 21 November 1964.

In its Introduction the decree said this:

> In recent times more than ever before, He [that is, God] has been rousing divided Christians to remorse over their divisions and to a longing for unity. Everywhere large numbers have felt the impulse of this grace, and among our separated brethren also there increases from day to day the movement, fostered by the grace of the Holy Spirit, for the restoration of unity among all Christians. This movement toward unity is called 'ecumenical.' Those belong to it who invoke the Triune God and confess Jesus as Lord and Saviour, doing this not merely as individuals but also as corporate bodies. For almost everyone regards the body in which he has heard the Gospel as his Church and indeed, God's Church. All however, though in different ways, long for the one visible Church of God, a Church truly universal and set forth into the world that the world may be converted to the Gospel and so be saved, to the glory of God.

And it went on to say:

> The Sacred Council gladly notes all this. It has already declared its teaching on the Church, and now, moved by a desire for the restoration of unity among all the followers of Christ, it wishes to set before all Catholics the ways and means by which they too can respond to this grace and to this divine call.

Documents and thinking such as this brought a wholly new warmth to Roman Catholic relations with other churches. Alongside this the slow commitments to conversation between the Church of England and the Methodist Church began to gather pace. Within the mainstream Reformed churches the foundations began to be laid for what became the United Reformed Church in 1972. Stuart Blanch became Bishop of Liverpool in 1966 and was fully committed to this springtime, building relationships of regular prayer with Archbishop

Beck and with the Methodist chair of district Rex Kissack, and in 1971 calling a joint Anglican-Methodist Synod to explore practical working.

Meanwhile in Bradford I was entering my teens, and this ecumenical springtime came into our own front room. The short ecumenical evangelism and nurture course 'The People Next Door' was launched across the churches in 1966. My parents hosted a group to engage with the course in our area. Ten years later that group was still going, and going strong, as ordinary Bradford Christians across the churches continued to learn from one another, to pray together and to dream of a church where all might be one.

Nationally the dream of unity was carried forward by the Anglicans and the Methodists as the 1960s drew to their close. Archbishop Michael Ramsey, himself the child of a Congregational home, lent his substantial weight to the venture. The aim was high – for a fully united church whose ministries would have been reconciled liturgically and sacramentally by a service which depended on its participants bearing with one another in love and saying and meaning words slightly differently for the sake of a future united people. Already the wider dream of united churches in England was being developed, the dream which would issue in the ecumenical commitment in 1964 that by 1980 the Anglican and the major free churches would have achieved an organic unity. Spring seemed to be turning into summer.

From all this the Roman Catholic church stood apart; yet since the conclusion of Vatican 2 the climate had changed irrevocably here also. As early as 1965 in Portsmouth the newly consecrated Bishop Derek Worlock, who of course had been present at all the sessions of the second Vatican Council as private secretary to the Cardinal Archbishop of Westminster, was initiating ecumenical conversation and partnership, readying himself as it were for the Liverpool years. And indeed the foretaste of ecumenical high Summer came to Liverpool with the Sheppard/Worlock partnership and with a united witness for the justice of the Kingdom and the friendship of the churches, which spoke to this city region and far beyond it. Archbishop Derek and Bishop David set a bar which remains in the minds and imaginations of a generation to this day.

When as new Bishop of Liverpool I attended the Civic Mass at the Metropolitan Cathedral earlier this year, and when Archbishop

Malcolm and I stood together to greet the people as they left at the end, I heard several times the whispered phrase 'fish and chips' – used constantly of David and Derek in their day – 'fish and chips: always together and never out of the papers!' John Newton, the great Methodist thinker and leader, in his time as Chair of Merseyside's free churches joined them on public platforms, contributed his own wisdom and theological acumen, and was accepted by the city region as the third leg of a tripod of growing unity which provided the platform from which the church's leadership could offer prophetic advice and practical wisdom far beyond the concerns of the churches for their own unity under God.

In 1975 I received my own vocation to the Anglican priesthood, and after looking at theological colleges in Oxford and Cambridge I decided to train for ministry at Queen's College Birmingham, the ecumenical foundation established, like Hope, from the coming-together of colleges, in the case of Queens Anglican and a Methodist theological college, and set up as a harbinger of a united training to come. So it was that I learned my Anglican church history from the Methodist tutor John Munsey Turner, my liturgics from an Orthodox layman, and my sacramental theology from a young Roman Catholic priest and teacher, at the time vice-principal of Oscott College, called Patrick Kelly. Patrick who, of course, later became Archbishop of Liverpool.

The achievements of the springtime years were substantial and as I have said, irrevocable. And yet, despite this, nationally over time the temperature began to cool. The Anglican/Methodist unity scheme of 1968 fell in 1969 in the Convocation and fell again in 1972 in the General Synod, on both occasions the councils of the Church of England rejecting the scheme despite Archbishop Ramsey's passionate advocacy. He saw it as the great failure of his archiepiscopate. Queen's Birmingham, far from being the first-fruits of a united future, became seen as a rather odd anomaly whose graduates were viewed quizzically by other Anglicans. The United Reformed Church indeed came into existence although rump churches remained outside that scheme, as they would have also outside any Anglican/Methodist united church. Then 1980 came and went with no further progress towards the unity which was so headily dreamed.

In short, ecumenism became an option rather than a mandate.

When my first daughter was baptised by a Methodist minister with whom I'd been at college, my bishop asked for an explanation. When I told him of our shared history at Queen's he simply said, 'Yes, we'd been wondering about that place'.

The establishment in the new towns of England of shared churches, including as a partner in many places the Roman Catholic church, went ahead in the 1980s with fanfare and great hope; when I was Bishop of Hertford I had to handle the sense in several of the churches of Stevenage, Hatfield and Hemel Hempstead that their brave new world was no longer valued by the wider church communities and that their forty years of faithful experiment would not be repeated. The Anglican/Methodist Covenant of 2003, about which I'll speak later, showed those churches a hopeful and practical way forward, but it was and is a far cry from Ramsey's vaulting hopes of a united people.

All this needs of course to be seen against the background of a rapidly-changing England. The Christendom of the 1950s had slowly been eroded in the 1960s and 1970s and the churches found that their place at the centre of society had become uncertain and contended. As we meet here today we can see how far, and how quickly, that process of change has gone and continues to go. It is not a crude secularism – very far from it – but it has made the platform of the churches into a very different thing from that inhabited by Pope John XXIII, or Archbishop Ramsey, or the Sheppard/Worlock partnership, or John Newton or Lord Donald Soper. Post-Christendom is our context now, and in such a world the demands on each Christian denomination to survive and thrive alone can all too easily take priority.

In which season are we now? The good news is that we are not and never will be back in the winter of the 1950s. The foundations laid by Stuart Blanch's generation, the achievements of the 60s and 70s abide; this University of course is one such. But nor are we in the Summertime. Rather to me it feels like Autumn, a season of mists, and not much mellow fruitfulness. For so many Christians today ecumenism has become a backdrop and as I say an option, not a mandate; and yet it also remains true that the prayer of our Lord at John 17:21 has not changed: that we may be one, as He and His Father are one.

And so as I have prepared this lecture, as I have looked at the horizons of ecumenism today I have asked myself, what will drive forward the work of the unity of the churches, in this odd and cool climate? What are the heartbeats of this endeavour for us in our time?

And I have come to believe that there are three modes of living as churches who seek unity, three ways in which we detect the heartbeat of God's desire for a people who are one; and they can be seen as the ecumenisms of blood, sweat and tears.

Blood

From Vatican radio, broadcast on February 16 this year (2015):

> Pope Francis on Monday denounced the murder of 21 Coptic Christians by ISIL militants in Libya. The Islamist terrorist organization released a video of the killings on Sunday.
> Speaking in Spanish to an ecumenical delegation from the Church of Scotland, the Holy Father noted those killed only said 'Jesus help me.'
> 'They were killed simply for the fact they were Christians,' Pope Francis said.
> 'The blood of our Christian brothers and sisters is a testimony which cries out to be heard,' said the Pope. It makes no difference whether they be Catholics, Orthodox, Copts or Protestants. They are Christians! Their blood is one and the same. Their blood confesses Christ.'

Pope Francis said that in remembering these brothers and sisters who have been murdered simply for confessing Christ, Christians should encourage one another in the ecumenical goal, noting the 'ecumenism of blood.' 'The martyrs belong to all Christians,' he said.

This was the first time I had heard the phrase, 'ecumenism of blood'. The Pope has since used it on a number of occasions, as the occasions of Christian martyrdom have increased in his time.

The ecumenism of blood, the red martyrdom of which the Celtic church spoke, is not to be sought masochistically, for its own sake.

In the first century St Ignatius of Antioch famously did seek it, and in his letter to the Romans insisted that he should find it:

Pardon me [in this]: I know what is for my benefit. Now I begin to be a disciple. And let no one, of things visible or invisible, envy me that I should attain to Jesus Christ. Let fire and the cross; let the crowds of wild beasts; let tearings, breakings, and dislocations of bones; let cutting off of members; let shatterings of the whole body; and let all the dreadful torments of the devil come upon me: only let me attain to Jesus Christ.

And later in that letter, and most famously, he said, 'Permit me to be an imitator of the passion of my God'.

This is a shocking and a challenging example, and yet Ignatius' example though debatably admirable is not to be followed. The ecumenism of blood is not indeed something to be sought, but is something given.

The fact of Christian faith places people in a situation which is wider and deeper than their Christian family, or tribe, or denomination. In a situation which can be settled, can be completed, without reference to denomination. Even when denomination is explicit, it is not relevant. It is reported that Father Maximilian Kolbe went to his death in Auschwitz, in the place of Franciszek Gajowniczek, with the words, 'I am a Catholic priest from Poland'. But he would not have been acquitted by his captors if he had been a Lutheran pastor. It was his status as 'Häftling', as prisoner, which defined him there. Similarly for the Lutheran Pastor Bonhoeffer in Flossenbürg. The ecumenism of blood does not operate in the arena of doctrinal discrimination, but of faithful witness.

For me all this has a wider application than the dreadful arena of violent death. For me, in the context of this enquiry, the ecumenism of blood stands as a sign of all those situations which are wider and deeper than the specifics of Christian membership or affiliation.

I spoke earlier of the Autumnal nature of the ecumenical endeavour in these days. In the face of disappointments in our structural relating, there has been both a prescinding and a settling – a prescinding from conversations about doctrinal and organisational/ecclesiological issues, and a settling for practical and social partnership in the service of the Kingdom.

I call this a settling, though in the scales of eternity it is the main thing. The so-called 'new ecumenism' in this England is not to be seen in committees of church leaders, nor in the Week of prayer for Christian Unity, but on the street in our foodbanks, our street pastors, our debt advice centres and credit unions, our addiction-recovery programmes and our political agitations. All this is martyrdom in the wide sense of the Greek *martus, martureo*, 'a witness', 'to witness'. It is Christian witnessing and almost always it prescinds from denomination.

An example of this from my own life. When I was a younger priest I acted for a while as co-chair of Christian CND and in this role each Ash Wednesday for a number of years I went with Christian friends to the Ministry of Defence, there to mark the building with ash and to pray for the nation, that we together might repent of our commitment to the threat of nuclear destruction, and might bring to our nation the possibility of that repentance and its impact on policy. These issues have not gone away in the decades since and indeed in this year, with the replacement of the Trident system on the political agenda, they have returned sharply.

But in sitting down in Whitehall, and in chaining myself to railings in Northolt, I sought to make a Christian and not an Anglican statement. And in the police cells in Cannon Row and in Watford, after I had been arrested, I sat with Catholics and Quakers indiscriminately; and I was not asked in the magistrate's court whether I was an Anglican; and if I had not been one, I would have been fined nonetheless.

Martyrdom is witness that is costly, and it is ecumenical of its nature. The only exceptions of course, and they are many, are the exceptions of blood martyrdom whereby we Christians have killed one another, or stigmatised or hurt or bitten or devoured one another, in the interests of our doctrines and of that cold truth which crushes human life. We may be proud of our martyrs, those who were killed in the name of Christ by other Christians; but we cannot commend their deaths to the world without shame.

And yet even this can give opportunity for redemption and mutual love and forbearance. Bishop Rowan Williams has written: 'You've... heard the words 'martyrial ecumenism,' and what they express is, to me, something utterly essential about the life of the Christian Church. From the moment when St. Paul recognized in Jesus the face of his victims, it has been a deep dimension of Christian holiness: to be able to go to one's brothers and sisters in repentance and receive from those whom we have offended or excluded the grace of God's welcome. When our churches learn to celebrate fully and gladly each other's martyrs—as they have begun to do—then that moment of Paul's conversion comes alive again.'

So even this kind of martyrdom can occasion for the whole Church repentance and recalling to Christ; and yet in the end it is not what the Pope means when he speaks of the ecumenism of blood, the red martyrdom.

The Celtic church, following indeed St Jerome, spoke also of a white martyrdom and of a 'glas' martyrdom – 'glas', a word than can mean blue or green, the colour of flesh under pressure, the colour of the flesh of the saints up to their necks in cold water and reciting the Psalter, the colour of costly witness, another colour of the ecumenism of blood. And yet as we see all these ways, death on the beach or chaining to railings or feeding the poor, as we recognise in them the heart of discipleship (or at least of the foolishness of God), as we reconfirm that they are the necessary and even the main thing, yet we must also recognise that they are not sufficient in the ecumenical endeavour. Because they all prescind from denomination, or settle for partnerships that undergird their co-operation without achieving unity, and they do not resolve the demands of our Lord's prayer in John 17:21, that we might be one. For this alongside blood there must be sweat, and also tears.

Sweat

The relationship between the ecumenism of blood and that of sweat has, of course, a rich history. In the years since the 1910 Edinburgh mission conference, the ecumenical work of the churches was divided into two streams, Faith and Order on the one hand, and Life and Work on the other. Life and Work has issued in the ecumenism of blood, and indeed Pastor Bonhoeffer was one of the leading lights of Life and Work in the years before the second world war. But it is Faith and Order that is called to enter the ecumenical sweatshop.

I have recently, at the invitation of the Archbishops of Canterbury and York, taken a responsibility as Anglican co-chair of the Joint Anglican-Methodist Covenant Advocacy and Monitoring Group, a catchy title I agree. As the name implies, it is a national bilateral body whose task is to advocate for ecumenical furthering, and to monitor its progress in the specific context of the Covenant between the Church of England and the Methodist Church; a Covenant which these churches entered in November 2003.

The Anglican-Methodist Covenant is a solemn agreement, but in keeping with the muted atmosphere of the ecumenical Autumn it is also a modest one. So, the Preamble to the Covenant is pretty robust:

> We the Methodist Church of Great Britain and the Church of England, on the basis of our shared history, our full agreement in the apostolic faith, our shared theological understandings of the nature and mission of the Church and of its ministry and oversight, and our agreement on the goal of full visible unity, as set out in the previous sections of our Common Statement, hereby make the following Covenant …

Modesty comes later. The Covenant document goes on to say that the Covenant is made 'in the form of interdependent Affirmations and Commitments'. These cover matters such as a mutual affirmation that '…in both our churches the word of God is authentically preached, and the sacraments of Baptism and the Eucharist are duly administered and celebrated', and a mutual commitment 'to listen to each other and to take account of each other's concerns, especially in areas that affect our relationship as churches'.

The subtlety of the choice of words, and in particular of verbs, in the Anglican-Methodist Covenant was the result of long and hard work, as ecumenically agreed documents have been through all the ages and between all the churches. Any one of these documents would illustrate the ecumenism of sweat. So for example two weeks ago the co-chairs of the International Commission for the Anglican-Orthodox Theological Dialogue presented the Archbishop of Canterbury and the Ecumenical Patriarch with a copy of the latest Agreed Statement, entitled *In The Image and Likeness of God: A Hope-Filled Anthropology*.

This document also could have formed the basis of this section of our enquiry, but I've chosen the Anglican-Methodist process because I know more about it and because on the face of it, moving it forward should be a simpler matter. After all John and Charles Wesley lived and died as Anglican priests, and the Methodist Church twice approved unity with the Church of England in the last fifty years. What could possibly go wrong?

From 2003 until this year the Covenant's implementation was overseen by a joint Anglican-Methodist commission called, inevitably, the Joint Implementation Commission or JIC. The JIC went through two incarnations before its life came to a natural end and the group of which I am now the co-chair succeeded it. In the interests of brevity I shall make an acronym of the Joint Anglican-Methodist Covenant Advocacy and Monitoring Group and will call it JCAMG. Alongside this is another bilateral group, this time including observers from the Roman Catholic, Baptist and United Reformed churches, called the Methodist-Anglican Panel for Unity in Mission, or MAPUM.

Now, friends, I am inflicting these acronyms and committees on you this evening for a purpose. Compared with the death of Christians in Libya, or the feeding of the poor in Liverpool, these committees and their work can seem extraordinarily rarified and irrelevant. And indeed they can sometimes be so. In any event, relevant or not, the ecumenism of sweat is an exacting business. Longfellow might have been thinking of this when he wrote: 'Though the mills of God grind slowly, yet they grind exceeding small; Though with patience He stands waiting, with exactness grinds He all.'

The patience of the Lord, or at any rate certainly the patience of the churches, has been sorely tried in the ecumenical process; and the inevitable temptation is to conclude that God is not interested in church unity if it comes at the price of so much tedium. But I believe that one of the heartbeats of ecumenism is precisely this exacting work of negotiation and theological exploration, and as Bishop of Liverpool I have given, and shall give, a fair portion of what you might call my allocated national working time to this belief, though my membership of the JCAMG group.

Think with me then, for a moment, in detail, about one aspect of what was done and what might be done in the Anglican/Methodist conversation, as an example of what the work of inter-church negotiation means and as a glimpse into the ecumenical sweatshop.

I said earlier that the fall of the Anglican-Methodist unity scheme was perceived by him as the great failure of the deeply distinguished archiepiscopate of Michael Ramsey. The scheme fell primarily because of doubts and questions, not only expressed within the Church of England but prevailing there, about two matters of ministry; the place of bishops in the Church, and the interchangeability of ministries between the Anglican and Methodist churches, in particular the interchangeability of presbyteral ministry. Put in the form of questions, we asked each other: 'Can Methodists please find a way to have bishops?' and, 'Can Anglicans please find a way to recognise the ministry of Methodists as they are?'.

Almost fifty years later these remain precisely the questions. When last year the JIC presented its final report to the Methodist Conference and the General Synod, it put the matter, with a refreshing and unusual asperity and frankness for an official report, like this:

> We are convinced that now is the time for both our churches to make bold initiatives which will break the logjam which is preventing the flourishing of our covenant relationship into… deeper communion. The two initiatives are closely connected and, ideally, would be made together.
>
> One initiative is in the hands of the Church of England. The Church of England needs to address the question of reconciling, with integrity, the existing presbyteral and diaconal ministries of our two churches, which would lead to the interchangeability of ministries.
>
> Addressing this question would take the affirmations of the Covenant concerning the ministries of our churches out of the realm of abstract theory and embody it in structures and practice … Such an initiative for reconciling existing presbyteral and diaconal ministries would be taken with the expectation of the Methodist Church taking a bold initiative in relation to personal episcopal ministry as described below.
>
> We also encourage the Church of England to take account of the existing theological agreement in essential doctrine with the Methodist Church and the affirmations about the Methodist Church and its ministries it has made in the Covenant Statement. It is important to recognise that proposals made previously for an act of reconciliation of ministries, which bears a resemblance to ordination, have been problematical not only for Methodists, but also to many in the Church of England …'

I shall return to this point in a moment.

The JIC report goes on:

> The other initiative is in the hands of the Methodist Church. The Methodist Church needs to address the question of expressing the Conference's ministry of oversight in a personal form of connexional, episcopal ministry (such as a President Bishop), in such a way that it could be recognised by the Church of England as a sign of continuity in faith, worship and mission in a church that is in the apostolic succession.
>
> Such a move would be on the basis of the Church of England making a bold initiative in relation to reconciling existing presbyteral and diaconal ministries, as described above.

These, then, are the questions which the Faith and Order specialists of the two churches are commissioned to explore, and which the JCAMG group is mandated to monitor.

You will remember that the JIC report made reference to an essential plank of the 1968 unity scheme, namely the mutual reconciliation of ministries at a liturgical service of worship which included a sacramental act which would have been both symbolic and performative.

In an earlier report the JIC noted that:

> [This service of reconciliation] was caught between some Methodists suspecting that what was proposed was re-ordination, and some Anglicans objecting because the act was ambiguous and therefore not sufficient in their eyes to give confidence that the ministry of Methodists was adequately ordered to officiate in the Church of England.

And it went on to say:

> The JIC recognises, sadly, that after fifty years, the dilemma seems as insoluble as ever. It is therefore keen to avoid raking over old coals ...'

The service of reconciliation would have involved the Methodist President and his senior colleagues as presbyters receiving the laying-on of hands with prayer from the Archbishop and other bishops, and the Archbishop and his colleagues in turn receiving the laying-on of hands from the Methodist President and his colleagues. It was roundly condemned from a number of quarters as a fudge and a disgracefully imprecise fudge at that. The previous Archbishop of Canterbury Geoffrey Fisher in a letter to the Times called it 'open double dealing'. So I can understand why in this generation it might be seen as an old coal best left alone.

The ecumenism of sweat may sometimes involve the raking over of old coals, however, and on behalf of JCAMG I have recently asked the national ecumenical officers of our two churches to re-examine this service of unity and to assess just how dead a duck it is. I shall also invite our Faith and Order people to do the same.

I have done and shall do this because I reread, in Owen Chadwick's magisterial biography of Archbishop Ramsey, Michael Ramsey's own defence of this service of reconciliation, and in reading it I was frankly inspired. A motif of this enquiry is that we do what we do for reasons of the heart as well as for reasons of analysis: 'Return empty to Scotland'. For reasons of the heart I have asked us to look again at this service, because speaking to the Diocesan Synod of the Canterbury Diocese in October 1968 Michael Ramsey said this:

> 'I know that I am a priest and a bishop in the historic order, referred to in our prayer book as coming down from the apostles' times. I know that Methodist ministers are ministers of the Word and sacrament used by Christ and they have been for many, many years. I know that their ministry is not identical with the historic episcopate and priesthood, but I am unable to define precisely what the relative value of the two is…
>
> 'Very well then. In this laying on of hands with prayers I would be asking God through His Holy Spirit to give to the Methodist ministers what He knows that they need to make their ministry identical with ours as presbyters and priests in the Church of God. It would be perfectly clear what was being asked for, the equalization of our ministries. What would be undefined and undefinable is the present relative status. For that there is a great deal of room for variety of opinion… The service asks God to be good enough to our ministries equal, giving to

them what grace and authority He knows that we need ...

'What would I mean receiving that laying-on of hands? I would mean this. I believe that I am a priest and a bishop in the Church of God. Nothing can make me more so. But I do believe that my ministry will have a very new significance and authority as a result of this Anglican-Methodist union, and I pray that God will give me that enrichment and significance through receiving the laying on of hands from the Methodist president and his colleagues.'

I remain sufficiently moved by this advocacy to ask the Church of England at least to revisit this dead duck and to see whether it might still have something to teach us. Because it points to a liturgical and not a confessional act, and it points to an apophatic confidence that the God whom we cannot understand will, in the mystery of His being and doing and out of His love for us, give us what we do not know we lack. It points in other words to a heartbeat of the spirit, and it can only be accessed in the sweatshop of ecumenical committees.

Finally on this, I quote again from a JIC report:

> The Anglican-Methodist Covenant is at a decisive moment. The JIC has kept in sight the crucial question as to whether there is evidence that the Covenant is making a difference. We have suggested that the criteria in this are the flourishing of the Kingdom and the greater unity of the Church, which are ultimately intrinsically intertwined. If the Covenant is to make a difference it must honour diversity, be purpose led, and place a high value on the coming of the Kingdom of God. It must assist in the discernment of the movement of the Kingdom and the dynamics of God's grace; and it must combine the energy and resources of our churches for the sake of mission.

All this is true and sets a proper perspective; and if there is to be progress in ecumenical partnership, and in paving a way for the unity of the churches, then the motives must be clear. The churches must be committed to the search for unity in order to see the mission of God and the Kingdom of God come closer. Within and as part of that search, the ecumenism of sweat is essential. On its own however it will never achieve anything, since (as the Roland Walls story at the beginning of this enquiry hoped to suggest) we do what we do, and the temperature of our commitment rises, for all sorts of reasons which include, but are by no means restricted to, committee reports.

A key part of our motivation is tied to the emotional longing with which the churches consider change, in this case the change that unity would bring. And we are called to raise that temperature, if we believe such change to be the will of God. For me this, more than anything else, is the role of JCAMG and of the ecumenical advocacy more generally. When we sweat it is because our temperature has been raised.

And yet to raise the temperature of the heart and of the churches, and to warm the climate of the ecumenical endeavour, cannot be a matter for sweat, for exhortation. Rather, the world will be changed by weeping. And the final, and the briefest, section of my enquiry speaks of weeping, of tears.

Tears

You have heard now of Roland Walls whose life changed as a result of seeing a train go by. He remained as an Anglican monk in Roslin for very many years, in a tiny community of three, four, at most five people, which sensed an ecumenical vocation even though they were all Anglican; and then something else happened to him.

Annually, he bought a Roman Catholic diary. In the front is a place where you write your name and that of a contact. The section reads 'I am a Catholic. In the event of an accident, please call a Priest'.

'I always used to cross out 'Catholic", said Roland, 'and I'd cross out 'Priest'. Instead I would write, "I am a Christian. In the event of an accident, please call another Christian".'

But in 1979, he said, when he bought his new diary and tried to make those amendments, his pen would not write. He thought it was just the pen malfunctioning. The following year, he got his new Catholic diary and found that, although his pen was working, he could no longer cross that sentence out. He wanted it to remain as it was. He then thought, 'That's strange. I must somewhere in myself want to die as a Catholic: and if I want to die as one, does that mean I ought to be living as one?'

This, together with feeling drawn to pray in Catholic churches while on his travels, brought Roland in the end to the doorstep of Cardinal Gray of Edinburgh to explore reception as a Catholic. At that doorstep Roland prayed, 'Lord, if this man talks to me about your Church, I shall know this is not from you. But if he talks about you and your Son then I shall know it is of you'.

The Cardinal shared with Roland his sense of the strangeness of this journey and then said this:

> This is not primarily about you, nor about your Church. It is about your Community. I would like you to go back to your Community and ask them one question. In their vocation to witness to the unity of the Church, are they prepared to undergo the pain of Christ at the Church's disunity – the sixth wound we inflict on the body of Christ – which your Community will experience at the Eucharist, like a sword piercing the heart of your Community's life? They must understand this as not just their own pain, but as the pain of Christ. This is a pain which I never feel, nor your own Church, as we all celebrate with our own. But your Community will experience this at each Eucharist.

We are told that the Cardinal went on to say this:

> The way forward to full unity will come only when the Church understands this: that the Eucharist is not only a joyful celebration of all that Christ has done and given us, but also displays the cost, the pain, that sixth wound, of which in practice we are not aware, celebrating separately in our own denominations. Yes, ecumenical conferences and dialogues are necessary and important... but they do not reach the heart of the matter, the pain of Christ, in the way your Community will.

We are told that the Cardinal then blessed Roland, and that as he rose from the blessing, he saw tears in the Cardinal's eyes.

And Roland went ahead and was received, and then ordained as a Catholic priest, and from that day the tiny Community at every Eucharist in their chapel was divided, as the whole Church is divided, and the pain of Christ was felt there as one or another stood and watched other receive the life of God and were unable themselves to receive.

Years later John Halsey, another member of the Community, said this:

> I don't think anyone chooses to experience pain for its own sake. So what has it been for, this pain at the Eucharist? Perhaps in some minute way we were able, through Roland's entry into the Roman Catholic Church and our consequent division, to help the whole Church to move together towards that unity for which Christ prayed and died.

The longing for unity expressed by Jesus in John 17:21 is rooted in tears. And without the heartbeat of tears the churches will never be one. I must say frankly that in these days, we weep insufficiently for Christ's broken body, the sixth wound. The ecumenical Autumn has frozen our tears, and we take for granted the parallel tracks of the church and the parallel contentments that come from a sundered body. In the ecumenism of blood we see the work of God realised as the unity of the church is proclaimed to a world that expects nothing else. But in my own work for unity in the realm of sweat, I know that the temperature of the churches has not risen enough to make the change. We have forgotten how to weep.

Here in Liverpool Hope University we see the future in stone. The walls that separated the two colleges on each side of this road are down, and the arch of the gospel has replaced them; the wall is down, as Shakespeare's Bottom the weaver says, the wall is down that parted their fathers.

But until the students and staff and visitors here, and in every church, walk through the arch and the door weeping for the broken body of the Lord, then we will not be one. We will settle for less. And so I end this enquiry with a plea for tears, for what the Orthodox call Penthos, for a gift of tears in and across the churches. It is not to be confused with depression, or with frustration, or with despair. It is a gift in the same way as the ecumenism of blood is a gift; a gift that motivates and changes, a gift of the Spirit. And I don't know how to pray for it, because who would ever have thought to pray in Roland Walls' case that his ballpoint pen should break down?

But the motivations of the Christian heart are manifold, and

God knows what is best for his Church. So in the end I simply pray that we remain discontented with what we have, and that we long for more; and that as Stuart Blanch did in his day we do what we can to stitch together the gaping wounds of Christ, and that as the present Archbishop of Canterbury says we might learn to disagree well, and perhaps one day to agree. It is those heartbeats for which I pray and for which I long; the heartbeats of ecumenism: blood, sweat and tears, the gifts of God to his people.

Appendix

These were the readings given by the Lectionary for my last day as Bishop in Liverpool. To them I have added a hymn I asked to be sung at my farewell service.

Psalm 45

Thy seat, O God, endureth for ever
  the sceptre of thy kingdom is a right sceptre.
Thou hast loved righteousness, and hated iniquity
  wherefore God, even thy God, hath anointed thee with the oil of gladness above thy fellows.
All thy garments smell of myrrh, aloes, and cassia
  out of the ivory palaces, whereby they have made thee glad.
Kings' daughters were among thy honourable women
  upon thy right hand did stand the queen in a vesture of gold, wrought about with divers colours.
Hearken, O daughter, and consider, incline thine ear
  forget also thine own people, and thy father's house.
So shall the King have pleasure in thy beauty
  for he is thy Lord God, and worship thou him.
And the daughter of Tyre shall be there with a gift
  like as the rich also among the people shall make their supplication before thee.

The King's daughter is all glorious within
  her clothing is of wrought gold.
She shall be brought unto the King in raiment of needle-work
  the virgins that be her fellows shall bear her company, and shall be brought unto thee.
With joy and gladness shall they be brought
  and shall enter into the King's palace.
Instead of thy fathers thou shalt have children

whom thou mayest make princes in all lands.
I will remember thy Name from one generation to another
therefore shall the people give thanks unto thee, world
without end.

A Reading from the Second Book of Chronicles

That night God appeared to Solomon, and said to him, 'Ask what I should give you.' Solomon said to God, 'You have shown great and steadfast love to my father David, and have made me succeed him as king. O Lord God, let your promise to my father David now be fulfilled, for you have made me king over a people as numerous as the dust of the earth. Give me now wisdom and knowledge to go out and come in before this people, for who can rule this great people of yours?' God answered Solomon, 'Because this was in your heart, and you have not asked for possessions, wealth, honour, or the life of those who hate you, and have not even asked for long life, but have asked for wisdom and knowledge for yourself that you may rule my people over whom I have made you king, wisdom and knowledge are granted to you. I will also give you riches, possessions, and honour, such as none of the kings had who were before you, and none after you shall have the like.' So Solomon came from the high place at Gibeon, from the tent of meeting, to Jerusalem. And he reigned over Israel.

Reading: John 16.23-end

Jesus said to his disciples, 'On that day you will ask nothing of me. Very truly, I tell you, if you ask anything of the Father in my name, he will give it to you. Until now you have not asked for anything in my name. Ask and you will receive, so that your joy may be complete.

'I have said these things to you in figures of speech. The hour is coming when I will no longer speak to you in figures, but will tell you plainly of the Father. On that day you will ask in my name. I do not say to you that I will ask the Father on your behalf; for the Father himself loves you, because you have loved me and have believed that I came from God. I came from the Father and have come into the world; again, I am leaving the world and am going to the Father.'

His disciples said, 'Yes, now you are speaking plainly, not in any figure of speech! Now we know that you know all things, and do not need to have anyone question you; by this we believe that you came from God.' Jesus answered them, 'Do you now believe? The hour is coming, indeed it has come, when you will be scattered, each one to his home, and you will leave me alone. Yet I am not alone because the Father is with me. I have said this to you, so that in me you may have peace. In the world you face persecution. But take courage; I have conquered the world!'

There's a wideness in God's mercy,
like the wideness of the sea;
there's a kindness in his justice
which is more than liberty.

There is no place where earth's sorrows
Are more felt than up in Heaven;
There is no place where earth's failings
Have such kindly judgment given.

There is welcome for the sinner,
And more graces for the good;
There is mercy with the Saviour;
There is healing in His blood.

For the love of God is broader
than the measure of our mind;
and the heart of the Eternal
is most wonderfully kind.

But we make His love too narrow
By false limits of our own;
And we magnify His strictness
With a zeal He will not own.

The Door

If our love were but more simple,
we should take him at his word;
And our lives would be all gladness
In the joy of Christ our Lord.

Frederick William Faber (1814-1863)

Notes

1. A Monk of the Eastern Church (Fr Lev Gillet), 'On the Invocation of the Name of Jesus', Fellowship of St Alban and St Sergius, 1949.
2. T. S. Eliot, 'Sweeney Agonistes', 1927.
3. 2 Corinthians 11:28.
4. Galatians 5:15.
5. Philippians 4:6.
6. John Macquarrie, *Principles of Christian Theology*, SCM Press 1966, p. 99. The phrase 'thrown possibility' is Heidegger's.
7. Acts 20:35, etc.
8. Ezekiel 34:16.
9. In other translations, for example the NRSV, Ezekiel 34:16 rather more ominously has 'I will strengthen the weak, but the fat and the strong I will destroy. I will feed them with justice.' So strong churches, too, will need to look out.
10. Ed Murrow, 'I Can Hear It Now' audio recording, 1941.
11. Martin Buber, *For the Sake of Heaven*, Atheneum Press, 1945.
12. See James Gleick, *Genius: the life and science of Richard Feynman*, Pantheon Books, 1992, p. 351.
13. For more on what sticks in the mind, see *Made to Stick* by Chip and Dan Heath, Random House, 2007.
14. See *The Table*, Darton, Longman and Todd, 2018.
15. They were: Psalm 45, 2 Chronicles 1:7-13, John 16.23-end. The readings are printed in the Appendx.
16. Revelation 3:20
17. C. S. Lewis, *Mere Christianity*, Geoffrey Bles, 1952, Book 3, Chapter 4.
18. John Drury, *The Pot and the Knife*, SCM, 1979, Foreword.

19 See for example pp. 48-49.
20 Dante Alighieri, 'Inferno', 1, 1.
21 Matthew 6:6.
22 David Brazier, *The New Buddhism*, Robinson 2001, passim.
23 *The New Buddhism*, p. 45.
24 Peter Brook, *The Empty Space*, MacGibbon and Kee, 1968, p. 136.
25 Rowan Williams, 23 July 2002.
26 See for example *Encountering the Depths*, Darton, Longman and Todd, 1981.
27 'His maternal grandfather was Sir Philip Crampton Smyly, honorary physician to Queen Victoria, and he was baptised by his mother's uncle, William Conyngham Plunket, archbishop of Dublin.'
28 For more on Fr Gilbert see the excellent biography by Rod Hacking, *Such a Long Journey*, Mowbray, 1988.
29 Hacking, *Such a Long Journey*, p. 47.
30 Rowan Williams, *The Wound of Knowledge*, Darton, Longman and Todd, 1990, p. 169.
31 Colossians 1:24.
32 Ruth Burrows OCD, *To Believe in Jesus*, Sheed & Ward, 1978, p. 1.
33 Ruth Burrows OCD, *Guidelines for Mystical Prayer*, Sheed & Ward, 1976, p. 88. Quoted in Rowan Williams, *The Wound of Knowledge*, p. 175.
34 *The Cloud of Unknowing and Other Works*, translated by A. C. Spearing, Penguin, 2001, pp. 44-45.
35 Matthew 6:6.
36 See 'The Prayer of the Poor', https://www.charlesdefoucauld.org/docs/6-the-pathway-of-prayer.pdf
37 See for example *The Spiritual Autobiography of Charles de Foucauld* (1964); *Charles de Foucauld*, Jaques Antier (1999).
38 In the chapter 'On ecumenism'.
39 See https://www.gaddesdenestate.co.uk/gaddesden-estate-history.
40 The story is told in John Miller, *A Simple Life*, St Andrew Press, 2014.

41 An example of those conversations is recounted in the preface to 'On ecumenism' below

42 Synopsis from Wikipedia, *A Night at the Opera* (film).

43 Peter Selby, *Liberating God*, SPCK, 1983, p. 94.

44 Al Barrett and Ruth Harley, *Being Interrupted*, SCM Press, 2020.

45 In *The Jesus Prayer* by Simon Barrington-Ward, BRF, 1996, p. 74. See also Archimandrite Sophrony, *The Monk of Mount Athos*, St Vladimir's Seminary Press, 1975.

46 John 1:18; 1 John 4:12.

47 In *Fairacres Chronicle*, Winter 1986.

48 See Roger Grainger, *The Drama of the Rite*, Liverpool University Press, 2008.

49 Colossians 3:3; 1 Corinthians 9:22.

50 Revelation 2:17.

51 *Summer Gifts* by Katharine Bayes (Kindle Direct Publishing).

52 Psalm 49:7-9, GNB.

53 John Macquarrie, *Principles of Christian Theology*, Revised Edition, SCM Press, 2003, p. 78. The word 'factical' is Macquarrie's.

54 John Austin Baker, *The Foolishness of God*, Darton, Longman and Todd, 1970.

55 Keith Ward, *The Concept of God*, Blackwell 1974, p. 160. Quoted in Geoffrey Lampe, *God as Spirit*, SCM Press, 1977, p. 44.

56 Psalm 30:11.

57 C. S. Lewis, *A Grief Observed*, Faber & Faber, 1961, p. 20.

58 Wilfrid Thesiger, *Arabian Sands*, Penguin Books, 1964, p. 83.

59 It is a harsh and a painful irony for me that I was away from home when Kate died, away for the first day in seventeen weeks, in Birmingham, visiting my old theological college to help with the appointment of a new Principal there.

60 I am sorry now that these people are all men, sorry that I did not listen harder in those years to the voices of other women beside Frances Young; to Judith Lieu and Helen Oppenheimer and Mary Daly and Carter Heyward. I am trying to learn now what I missed then. And I am sorry now that they were all white, sorry that I did not listen harder in those years to the voices of people of colour, to James Cone and Tissa Balasuriya and Kosuke Koyama. I am trying

to learn now what I missed then.

61 John Robinson, *The Human Face of God*, SCM Press, 1973, p. 211.
62 John Robinson, *Honest to God*, SCM Press, 1963, pp. 52-3.
63 John Robinson, *The Difference in Being a Christian Today*, Fontana, 1974, p. 29.
64 T. S. Eliot, 'The Journey of the Magi', 1927.
65 J. G. Davies, *Every Day God: Encountering the Holy in World and Worship*, SCM, 1973.
66 'The Piper at the Gates of Dawn', in *The Wind in the Willows*, Kenneth Grahame, Methuen, 1908.
67 Martin Buber, *Between Man and Man*, Kegan Paul, 1947.
68 The story is told in Aubrey Hodes, *Encounter with Martin Buber*, Penguin Books, 1971, pp, 18-19.
69 Martin Buber, *Ich und Du* (*I and Thou*), originally published 1923. English translation by Walter Kaufmann, 1970.
70 See e.g. John Wimber, *Power Evangelism*, Hodder & Stoughton, 1997. Wimber was using the ideas of Thomas Kuhn, whose book *The Structure of Scientific Revolutions* coined the paradigm-shift phrase.
71 Maurice Wiles, *Faith and the Mystery of God*, SCM Press, 1982.
72 John 20:17.
73 The word 'demonised' is simply a transliteration of the biblical δαιμονίζομαι (*daimonizomai*), see e.g. Matt. 8:16, Mk 1:32, Luke 8:36, etc.
74 Mark 5:15
75 Walter J. Hollenweger, *Pentecost Between Black and White: five case studies on Pentecost and politics*, Christian Journals Ltd, Belfast, 1974.
76 Ted Hughes, 'Song for a Phallus' in *Crow*, Faber & Faber, 1970.
77 See the short chapter 'On conversion therapy' below, for a little more on this.
78 2 Corinthians 5:7.
79 John 2:17.
80 By one of our teachers, Mark de Rond, Professor of Organizational Ethnography at Cambridge University [Judge Business School].

81 See 'On love and anger' later in this volume.

82 Quoted in David Mamet, *True and False*, Faber & Faber, 1998, p.25.

83 See Horst Rittel and Melvin Webber, 'Dilemmas in a General Theory of Planning', Policy Sciences 4, 1973, pp. 155ff.

84 https://www.belfasttelegraph.co.uk/news/northern-ireland/how-martin-mcguinness-and-ian-paisley-forged-an-unlikely-friendship-35550640.html

85 Oliver Cromwell, letter 129, to the General Assembly of the Kirk of Scotland, August 1650.

86 Bishop Mariann Edgar Budde, *How We Learn To Be Brave*, Authentic Media, 2023.

87 Matt. 10:18, 19.

88 For the benefit of any reader under 50, Don's was a popular voice in the 1980s, especially through his TV series *The Sea of Faith* and his many books advocating a non-realist understanding of God.

89 Don Cupitt, *The World To Come*, SCM Press, 1982.

90 Don Cupitt, *Taking Leave of God*, SCM Press, 1980.

91 Don Cupitt, *Mysticism after Modernity*, Blackwell, 1998.

92 Isaiah 55:9-11.

93 Goro Shimura speaking of Yutaka Tanayama, in Simon Singh, *Fermat's Last Theorem*, Fourth Estate, 1997, pp. 194ff. See also BBC Horizon documentary, 1996.

94 Desmond Tutu, *God is Not a Christian*, HarperOne, 2011.

95 Richard Holloway, *Leaving Alexandria*, Canongate Books, 2012.

96 David Jenkins obituary, *Church Times*, 6 September 2016.

97 In F. A. Iremonger, *William Temple*, OUP, 1948, p. 162.

98 See http://thelarkintrail.co.uk

99 Quoted in Andrew Motion, *Philip Larkin: A Writer's Life*, Faber & Faber, 1993, p. 486.

100 Larkin, 'Aubade', 1977, uncollected.

101 Quoted in Andrew Motion, *A Writer's Life*, p. 274.

102 Quoted in Andrew Motion, *A Writer's Life*, p. 371.

103 Andrew Motion, *A Writer's Life*, pp. 274-5.

104 Henry Williamson, *The Gale of the World*, Macdonald, 1969.

105 Herbert McCabe, *The Teaching of the Catholic Church: A New Catechism of Christian Doctrine*, Darton, Longman and Todd, 2000.

106 Herbert McCabe, *On Aquinas*, Burns & Oates, 2008, p. 167.

107 Gordon W. Lathrop, *Holy Ground: A Liturgical Cosmology*, Fortress Press, 2009, pp. 64-5.

108 Daniel Berrigan SJ, *America is Hard to Find*, SPCK, 1973.

109 http://www.unadulteratedlove.net/blog/2018/1/27/fr-bill-kirkpatrick-rip

110 https://www.channel4.com/4viewers/blog/its-a-sin

111 https://www.theatlantic.com/daily-dish/archive/2009/06/for-hard-core-petheads-the-tennant-interview-in-full/200905/

112 For example *The Creativity of Listening: Being There, Reaching Out, AIDS: Sharing the Pain,* and *Going Forth: a practical and spiritual approach to dying and death.*

113 https://www.barnesandsons.co.uk/news/the-late-father-william-john-ashley-kirkpatrick-father-bill/

114 See https://rebellion.earth/the-truth/demands/

115 Extinction Rebellion, *This Is Not A Drill*, Penguin Books, 2019.